I0417257

Butterfly

Happiness is like a butterfly which, when pursued, is always beyond our grasp, but, if you will sit down quietly, it may alight upon you.

Nathaniel Hawthorne

1 Las Casas

The two men talked in hushed tones, although their footsteps on the stone flags echoed in the narrow corridor, along either side of which were three steel doors with observation flaps. They stopped at the last door on the left. The Englishman, Ralph, spoke first, his voice and accent attesting to an expensive education at the best schools and, some would argue, the best university, "So this is where you have him; I must say it's suitably mediaeval."

The American, Jack, who was very fat, replied in a southern drawl, attesting to a chaotic education in several expensive southern schools and three years spent in an alcoholic haze at Yale, "We're well below street level. Notice the silence; no traffic noise and nobody can hear a sound coming from here."

Ralph raised his eyebrows, the same colour as his thin blond hair and consequently hardly apparent; his blue eyes twinkled, "No point in disturbing the neighbours; not that I would indulge in anything untoward, myself: I still believe in the essential goodness of man and that monstrous treatment produces monsters."

Jack's brown eyes were unsmiling, reminiscent of those of a dead fish. "I can't say the same for our hosts: they enjoy beating the living daylights out of their prisoners and have an inventory of tortures that the Spanish Inquisition would envy. You can observe our guest through the grill."

Ralph slid back the well-oiled flap and peered into the cell, which was brightly lit by a single bulb in the ceiling.

Jack hitched up his pants, which were overhung by his stomach. "What's he doing?"

"He's sitting against the wall with his hands on his knees. His eyes are closed, but he isn't asleep: his right forefinger is tapping his knee."

"I guess he's listening to music in his head; he only stops tapping when he sleeps."

"He sleeps in that position?"

"He must find it more comfortable than lying on the concrete floor."

"He was in some tough places in his younger days; that's a position the Viets assume when resting. How long has he been there?"

"Since eight o'clock yesterday."

Ralph looked at his watch. "Twenty-four hours. Has he had food and water?"

"No. And we cleared the cell, except for the bucket in the corner. The guards have orders to rattle the door and switch the light off and on at irregular intervals."

"And you think he managed to sleep?"

"I'm convinced he did."

Ralph closed the flap silently. "So much for sleep deprivation."

Jack wiped sweat from his forehead with a not too clean handkerchief. "Has he had training?"

Ralph thought for a moment. "I don't know; but on one of our discreet searches of his accommodation, we found a book 'Battle for the Mind'."

"I have the same; it's hardly incriminating."

"No. But he must know what we are up to. Where's the interview room?"

"Just down the corridor. Don't be fooled by the location; the room is state of the art; there's an observation booth behind one-way glass and it has CCTV to record the interviews."

"Is that a good idea? Why commit them to tape?"

"We like to study the tapes and use them for training our people. We always edit them."

"Who gets to have first go at him?"

"Maria. She's an MD with psychiatric training. She can charm the birds from the trees: her bedside manner usually works better than our cruder methods, but we can always fall back on them if her charm fails."

A woman in a white coat came down the steps leading to the underground cells. Of obvious mixed race, she had short, black hair and the figure and complexion of a typical Mayan peasant, habituated to hard work in intemperate weather.

"Here's Maria, bearing food and drink for our guest."

She balanced a tray on her on her left hand, like one accustomed to serving meals and raised her right hand in greeting. "Room service. Hello Jack."

"Hi! Maria, this is Ralph; he's the MI6 guy who asked us to pick up our guest."

"Hello, Ralph. The file you sent us is very interesting: either this man is innocent or a very clever sleeper."

"I'm delighted to meet you, Maria. I can assure you …"

Maria raised her right hand. "Don't tell me; I like to make up my own mind. I'll wait in the interview room. Could you have the guard bring him to me? You shouldn't show yourself, Ralph; we need to keep you for later."

Jack took Ralph's arm. "We'll go to the observation room: we can watch the interview from there."

Maria was waiting behind a table in the interview room when the prisoner was brought in by a guard. In spite of his long hair and beard, it was obvious that he had been beaten about the face. Maria motioned to a chair at the other side of the table.

"Good morning, Mr Armstrong; please sit down. My name is Maria Ruiz."

Brian made no reply. He sat down and stared at the woman: she reminded him of someone but it was only later that he remembered who.

"Why the white coat? Are you a doctor?"

"Yes, I am. Does my white coat bother you?"

"No. I could do with a doctor."

Maria smiled and Brian saw that she was beautiful.

"Tell me, Brian, I may call you Brian?"

"Please yourself."

"Tell me, Brian, why are you in our country?"

"Before I answer any questions, I want to know why I am here."

"You are aware, Brian, that we are living in troubled times. We have to protect our borders."

"Protect your borders? I came here legally. What right had those thugs to drag me off the street and bring me here? I want to talk to my consul."

"And what would you tell your consul?"

"That I was mugged, beaten up and kidnapped."

Maria smiled indulgently. "I know exactly what the consul would say. He would tell you that you were lucky; if you had been mugged, your attackers would have stabbed or shot you first and then robbed you.

"So I'm lucky, am I? You can see what they did to my face, not to mention the bruises you can't see."

"You resisted arrest, Brian. I can't see much of your face. Why the long hair and beard?"

"It's a cunning disguise."

"Don't be flippant; this is a serious matter; why did you resist arrest?"

"They were in plain clothes."

"Now what use is a policeman in uniform? A criminal would be on his guard and a man in uniform would be in danger."

Brian flopped back in his chair. "I'm not a criminal; I thought I was being mugged."

"And you fought back; one of them has a black eye. They had to restrain you."

"Is that what you call it? You still haven't answered my question: why am I here?"

Maria pulled the tray into the middle of the table; there was a bottle of water and a dish of tortillas on it. "You know why you are here. Are you thirsty, Brian?"

"Yes. I've had nothing since yesterday morning."

"Have this water and some tortillas."

Brian picked up the bottle of water and looked at the seal.

"It's just mineral water, Brian; the bottle is sealed."

Brian cracked open the seal and sipped the water. Behind him, there was a mirror, which went the width of the wall. Behind that, Jack and Ralph observed the scene. In spite of the sound proofing, which made it unnecessary, Jack whispered, "He's a cool customer. Notice how he is sipping the water."

Ralph nodded and spoke in a normal voice. "He's dehydrated. I'd swear he has been trained; he's not going for the tortillas."

Maria pushed the dish of tortillas towards Brian. "You must be hungry; these tortillas are still warm from the oven."

Brian did not answer. Maria took a tortilla. "No? I haven't had breakfast. I'll have one."

Ralph nudged Jack. "He's very hungry but he's ignoring the food."

Jack mopped his brow. In spite of being underground, the room was hot. "Perhaps you're right; he may have had training. Wait a moment."

Brian took a tortilla from the dish and tore off a piece.

-That's right, Brian. Eat.

Because his mouth was full of food, Brian croaked, "I want to call my consulate.

Impatiently, Maria said, "After we have had our talk. I have your file here."

Brian swallowed and said, "What!"

"It's your curriculum vitae, Brian; it makes very interesting reading."

"I'm not saying another word until I've seen my consul."

Maria stood up, took the file and banged on the door. "Very well Brian, I'll ask your consul to come here."

"Thank you. You are too kind."

"You'll have to go back to your cell while I make the arrangements."

As Brian was being led back to his cell, he remembered who it was that Maria reminded him of.

2 Hanoi

The ward was quiet. Overhead fans stirred the humid air and slats of bright sunshine pierced the louvered windows. Then there was a creaking of bedsprings as the men turned to look at the girl who had come in: she was small, slim, but well-proportioned and obviously Eurasian, the fruit of the union of France and Vietnam. The ward sister pointed to Brian and the girl walked purposefully towards him; she stopped at his bedside.

"Are you awake? I think you are. You opened your eyes: you saw a beautiful woman and thought you were in heaven, n'est-ce pas?"

Brian levered himself up on his elbow and winced with pain.

"I know I'm not in heaven because my leg hurts like hell. But you are beautiful."

"Shall I call the nurse?"

"No need. If they give me any more morphine, I'll be an addict."

She smiled. Her smile was as disturbing as the perfume she exuded. "Quite right. There are too many drug addicts in Hanoi as it is. They think a pipe or two will solve their problems, but it never does. Let me introduce myself. I'm Sylvie; I'm famous for being naughty and also being the sister-in-law of Paul Guinet, the richest man in Hanoi. I visit our brave legionnaires to cheer them up; it's your turn today. Some are injured like you; some are bursting with health and much more amusing."

"And I'm Brian, better known as Rosbif in the Legion."

"You're English. How romantic. Did you join the Legion to forget?"

"No. I was on the run."

She put her hand to her mouth in feigned horror.

"You did something terrible."

"It's a long story."

She leaned forward and Brian forgot the pain in his leg.

"I love long stories."

"You'll be bored"

"No, I won't, I'm something like a sister confessor: the boys all tell me their sad stories; how they were wrongly accused of robbing a bank or killing a policeman, then they ask me for a date."

She pulled a chair to the bedside.

"Now I'm sitting comfortably, you can begin. Telling me about the terrible things you have done will take you mind off your pain."

"If you insist."

"I insist."

"I was seventeen and I had just finished secondary school; I had taken the final exams but I hadn't had the results. We had a small farm and there was a lot to do. One Sunday morning, I slept too long; I was supposed to feed the animals. At seven o'clock I was still asleep when my father came into my room, threw the bedclothes off me a laid into me with his belt."

"So you killed him."

"No, but I felt like it. I got up and did my work. Later that day, Sunday being a day of rest, I was leaning on my shovel during a pause in cleaning out the animals, when I felt a huge blow from his stick across my back. It was so painful that I couldn't breathe for a few seconds. I turned and saw him: he had a mad look in his eyes. I swung the heavy shovel; it was caked with pig shit and when it landed on his head, he crashed to the floor. I looked down at him; his head was liberally bemerded, his nose was oozing blood."

"So you did kill him."

"No. But I knew that once he came round he would kill me. The doctor came and he was carted off to hospital. The police came and took my statement. They were very understanding: they said they'd make sure I got at least two years in jail or maybe more if they could make attempted murder stick."

"So you ran."

"I ran. I had a passport and I knew where my father kept his cash. I took enough to get me to Paris. I went to Dover where I caught a ferry to Calais. On the train to Paris, I found a leaflet lying on the bench; it was about the Legion. I went to the recruiting office in Paris and finished up in Sidi-bel-Abbes."

"That was a very rash thing to do. Did you know anything about the Legion?"

"Only what I'd seen in the movies."

Sylvie laughed. "The Legion is nothing like the movies."

"I knew that."

"It is full of Germans: SS and death camp guards, war criminals, running for their lives."

"I found that out later."

"And a handsome young man like you is in danger from perverts. Some of them have been known to rape chickens."

Brian grimaced at a memory.

"I found that out quickly enough and it almost cost me my life. There was a German called Frank. He came on to me and when I told him to piss off, he turned nasty and said he might just kill me."

"Then you almost got killed at Dien Bien Phu. The Legionnaires have a tradition of carelessly throwing way their lives. That's the origin of their famous slow march which they do that while approaching the enemy. It's unbelievable but do you know that the Legionnaires in Hanoi are volunteering to parachute into Dien Bien Phu? They know the place is bound to fall but they say they want to be with their comrades."

"I think that's a noble thing to do."

"And I think it's a stupid thing to do; they will be killed or captured."

"The Legion has its traditions; loyalty is one of them."

"And stupidity is another. You were a silly boy: you should have stayed in Paris and found a high class lady to support you."

Brian grinned. "That position is still open."

"And I'm not applying for it. Do you read?"

"Yes. I like reading and I've plenty of time to do it in here."

"Can you read French?"

"Yes. I studied French and I've learnt a lot in the Legion, especially vulgar words and slang."

"Then you'll enjoy the San-Antonio books: they're very slangy, very rude and very popular. I'll come tomorrow. I must go and get ready for a party Paul Guinet is giving."

Brian was incredulous.

"Do people still have parties?"

"Armageddon is about to hit us: it's the best possible time to have parties. Once the communists take over, Hanoi will be dead; and wasn't it a British tradition to have a ball before a battle?"

"I believe there was one before Waterloo. But we were fighting the French and victory was assured. What's Paul like?"

Sylvie stood up and smoothed her dress over her slim hips. The soldiers in the nearby beds who had been listening and watching her intently, groaned in unison.

"Paul is short, fat, and lecherous, but he gives wonderful parties."

3 Las Casas

Jack leaned back in his chair, put his feet in his desk and folded his hands on his stomach. Ralph, who occupied the one comfortable armchair in the room, pointed to Jack's distended abdomen.

"You've got what the French call 'a colonial egg', Jack."

Jack was not pleased. "Since I carry it around, I am well aware that I am far from sylphlike, but I don't need a Limey to remind me."

Ralph was penitent. "Sorry, Jack. You know, I'm very keen on tennis: we should play while I am here."

"If we had a court, we could play, but there isn't one within a hundred miles, so I'll just have to keep my colonial egg."

Maria came in carrying Brian's file and Jack resumed the vertical.

"Well, Maria, what do you think?"

"We'll have to be careful: he tries to give the impression that he is in command of himself, but his body language tells me that he has a violent temper."

"We have two policemen who will vouch for that."

Ralph stood up and paced the room.

"I presume that I am to play the role of the consul."

Maria quickly sat in the armchair and gave Ralph a broad smile.

"Yes, Ralph. You are perfect for the part."

"I have never met Brian, but I feel I know him very well. I have been collating watchers' reports on him for the last five years. What about you, Jack?"

"I've read the file: there's a lot of circumstantial stuff, but nothing specific."

Ralph stood up. "That's the point: there's so much circumstantial stuff that I felt we had to pull him in."

"Why haven't you done it before?

"Well, Maria, several of our watchers have talked to him casually, usually in bars when he had been drinking. After a few drinks, he is easily provoked into giving a lecture on inequality and injustice in the world, but he's never given us a compelling reason to arrest him."

"Then why detain him now?"

Ralph leaned against the windowsill and gazed at the distant mountains.

"He was in the mountains between here and Tuxtla for two weeks. You know as well as I do that the situation is volatile: something big is going down, but we are not sure what."

"And you think he might be able to enlighten us?"

"Possibly. When do I perform as the consul?"

"Tomorrow."

Jack leaned back in his chair. "What regime do you recommend, Maria? Do we continue as we started?"

"He isn't the kind to be easily intimidated. I suggest we put him in the VIP accommodation."

Jack explained. "It's where we put the important drug traffickers, Ralph: comfortable bed, en-suite bathroom, TV, magazines."

"For drug barons?"

Jack's dead-fish eyes came to life for a moment. "Only the big ones. We show them the usual, bare cell. Then in time-honoured fashion, we show them the instruments. Finally we show them the VIP suite and give them a choice: collaborate and they get the Ritz; clam up and they go back to the days of the Spanish Inquisition."

Ralph was doubtful. "Does it work?"

"They sing like canaries. The fact is, they know much more about what's happening in this country than we do. They give us the dirt on a surprising number of politicos; most of them are up to the neck in corruption."

Maria explained the next move. "If they collaborate completely, they get to go to the Country Club."

Ralph was intrigued. "And what is the Country Club?"

"It's a ranch with round-the-clock protection: the guests have everything they could want except freedom of movement."

Jack flopped back into his chair. "Which they don't want; they'd be dead within days if they left our tender care."

Brian was sitting at the table in the interview room facing the mirror. He stared at his reflection, thinking, "If I am going to be a movie star, I really should get a haircut."

Maria came in with Ralph, who was carrying a smart, designer briefcase.

"Your consul to see you, Brian; I'll leave you to talk."

Maria glanced at Ralph and then at Brian before going out. Ralph took the chair facing Brian and placed his briefcase carefully on the table.

"Good morning. I'm sorry I took so long to come."

"Better late than never."

"I asked to see you as soon as I heard you were here, but they wouldn't let me. How are they treating you?"

"The first twenty-four hours were uncomfortable; then they moved me to a five-star suite: they even brought my things from my hotel. I've been able to shower and change."

"I'm glad. What happened to your face?"

Brian touched his eye gingerly. "I was *restrained* by the plainclothes policemen who abducted me."

Ralph's voice was unctuous, soothing, mellifluous, and, Brian found, annoyingly effeminate. "I'm really sorry. The police here tend to be rather heavy handed. Do you know why you were arrested?"

"I have no idea."

Ralph took a notebook from his briefcase and carefully aligned a pen next to it.

"I need a few basic facts. What is the purpose of your visit to Las Casas?"

"I'm a tourist."

"But this is hardly tourist country, Brian: it can be very dangerous."

"You don't have to tell me."

"Then why did you take the risk?"

Ralph's motherly concern was starting to annoy Brian. "I'm interested in geology and I collect gemstones. Some people collect stamps; I collect semi-precious stones. I was touring the old mining towns and adding to my collection. You can pick up specimens very cheaply here."

"I see. Apart from the mining towns, where did you go?"

"I did the Mayan temples bit and went up into the mountains."

"Why the mountains?"

"Mountains do have a certain interest for amateur geologists."

"I suppose they do, but rumour has it that there is some guerilla activity in the mountains."

"I wasn't aware of that."

"Did you see anything out of the ordinary?"

"Not a thing."

"What about the Indians?"

"They were very friendly. The only problem was the moonshine they plied me with."

"*Pulque*. It packs a punch."

"And it leaves you with a terrible hangover."

Ralph leaned forward, a serious look on his face. "Now I'll be straight with you, Brian; if I am to help you, you must confide in me: anything you say will be in strict confidence. The people upstairs tell me you have been on a watch list for a number of years. Why is that?"

Brian sat bolt upright and looked straight into Ralph's blue eyes. "I'm aware of being watched. You have no idea how stupid the so-called intelligence operatives are. I have had hours of amusement, usually in bars, stringing them along with tales of what will happen when the revolution comes."

"And what will happen?"

Brian's voice was ice and he articulated slowly and deliberately. "We'll take people who pretend to be consuls, put them against a wall and pretend to shoot them. Then we'll put them to useful work like sweeping the streets and collecting garbage. Garbage collection is all they are qualified for: they have spent their working lives doing it. This interview is over."

Ralph was aghast. "I say! How am I to help you if you refuse to talk to me? I can assure you..."

"Sod off!"

"Very well, if that's your attitude, I'll leave you to the tender care of your hosts."

In the observation room, Maria looked at Jack. "Oh dear! Ralph has blown it. He's about as subtle as a bull in a china shop."

"He will never trust us now. I'll get the guards to take him back to his cell."

"The VIP suite?"

"Yes, Jack. And I think you should take the next session."

"That suits me fine, but I'm tempted to have him softened up first."

"No, Jack. That's exactly what he is expecting after his latest performance. Let's surprise him. Anyway, he's a tough nut: you can't spend five years in the Legion if you are soft."

4 Sidi-bel-Abbes

Sidi-bel-Abes was the town built by the Legion. That day, it was humming with activity; heat and flies and dust devils swirled across the parade ground. The next Indochina draft was in the process of being assembled. The sun was relentless and Brian was sorry he had swung that shovel and run. The drill sergeants were chosen for their sadistic nature and, for six weeks, Brian had been given the full treatment. In the canteen, he collected rice and meat, the usual fare, from the counter, added bread, a bottle of *rouge* and a bowl of yogurt to the tray and made his way to an empty chair next to his German friend, Gunter.

"Heard the news, Brian?"

"What news?"

Gunter grinned as he broke off a piece of bread. "They're sending us to Indochina."

"I heard the rumour: the sergeant said De Lattre has asked for more troops."

"He's getting us and he has faith in the Legion. The war is going badly, with Mao's army is on the frontier and the French Expeditionary Force in retreat. De Lattre has been sent to stop the rot, so we're going to Tonkin."

Brian ate hungrily; there was nothing like square bashing for giving you an appetite. He had lost several pounds during his training and his muscles had been toned up. He had to admit that he had never felt better.

"What's it like in Tonkin, wherever that is?"

"It's in northern Indochina and, according to the sergeant, it's a green hell. Where it's not jungle, it's flooded paddy fields. He says he spent most of his time there covered in mud. He says the communists dress in black and sink into the slime then they suddenly stand up and blow you away."

"That's nice to know, but I won't be sorry to leave Sidi-bel-Abbes: all sand, heat and flies."

"Well, we're going to Tonkin: all mud, heat and mosquitoes. I don't like the idea of this war."

"Why is that?"

"Indochina is a colony; the Vietminh are not going to thank us for helping the French colonists: they want their country back."

"The whole purpose of the Legion is to fight colonial wars: we joined up, so we have to face the fact that we won't be welcomed as liberators."

Gunter's expression was serious. "I learnt that lesson the hard way. I was seventeen in 1944: we had lost the war, but I was given a uniform and a rifle and sent to Lyon. It's funny how names come round: it was the month before de Lattre arrived to liberate the city. The French Resistance was very active: they tossed a grenade into a café used by our officers and four died. The Gestapo pulled four Frenchman out of the Villeurbanne jail and we shot them in front of the café. I remember it was called Le Moulin a Vent. It was a nightmare; I was detailed for the firing squad and we were ordered to shoot the men in the stomach."

"So they didn't die quickly?"

"They took hours. I can tell you I was scared to death. I pulled my helmet as far down my forehead as I could. We all knew the war was lost and the French would take their revenge."

"I saw newsreels of the Resistance killing collaborators."

"They were machine gunned as soon as they were caught. We surrendered to De Lattre and were put in a prison camp. I saw a guard reading a Lyon paper: there was a photo of a woman with a shaven head on the front page. What would they have done to me if they had known I was at the Moulin a Vent? I hardly slept until we were sent back to Germany."

"After that experience, why did you enlist in the Legion?"

"I went back to Hamburg. The family house, along with most of the city, had gone. The city authorities had a rebuilding plan ready: thanks to the British Royal Air Force, they were able to incorporate plenty of green spaces. If we had won the war, we would have tried the Allied leaders for war crimes. Carpet bombing of civilian centres is a war crime. The fire-bombing of Dresden was especially wicked: a beautiful city burnt down and most of the population incinerated or boiled to death when they jumped into the River Elbe. The war was over and Dresden had no war industries: it was willful mass murder."

"Let's not get into the massacre of civilians: it happened on both sides. When a war ends, it's the losers who get punished. Did you stay in Hamburg?"

"No. My parents had moved to a mining town in the Ruhr. I joined my father in a coal mine; t was a good move: we were well paid and got extra rations."

"But you got tired of the mine."

"Yes. It's not a career. I took a holiday in Paris."

"That was a reckless thing to do."

"Not at all. I was surprised how readily the French had forgiven us. I realized there had been so many collaborators that talking about the war was taboo. I happened to come across the Legion Recruitment Office and I just walked in.

-Did you tell them what you had done in the war?"

"I didn't mention the Moulin a Vent. What about you?"

"I forgot to mention that the British police were after me for hitting my father with a shovel; I just said I fancied the glamour and adventure of the Legion: they laughed like hell at that, but they let me in."

"They are desperate for Indochina cannon fodder."

"Is it as bad as that?"

"The situation is completely chaotic: the Viets don't want to fight the communist Vietminh. If they don't want to fight for their own country, how can we or the French help them?"

"I think we are going to find out."

"I have some more bad news for you: Frank, the pervert, is coming with us."

"He keeps saying what he is going to do to me."

"He's a psychopath: he was SS during the war. They say he was a guard at one of the extermination camps."

"Our government kept those quiet; we only heard about them after the war."

"They didn't want to add to your worries."

"What should I do about Frank? Should I report him?"

"That's the last thing to do. You could challenge him to a knife fight, but you would lose. I'll watch your back; the Legion takes care of its own and the Legion will take care of Frank."

A heavy silence fell over the town as Brian made his way back to his barracks to fall into his bed and forget.

5 Las Casas

Brian was in the interview room. Jack came in, sweating profusely, sat down and mopped his neck.

"Did you sleep well, Brian?"

"Like a top."

"Did you enjoy last night's dinner?"

"It was very good."

"And breakfast?"

"First class."

"I'm glad you are enjoying your stay."

"I didn't say that."

"No. You must be wondering when you are going to be released."

"Yes. When is this nonsense going to stop?"

"You didn't help your cause when you insulted the consul."

Brian was angry. "Consul, my foot. If he's the consul, I'm Che Guevara."

"We know you aren't Che Guevara. Why did you pick on that name?"

"No reason. He just happens to be dead."

In the observation booth, Ralph leaned towards Maria and whispered, "Freudian slip?"

"No. He's taunting us: he knows he is being observed."

In the interview room, Jack leaned back in his chair and slackened his belt a notch.

"What makes you doubt that the man who interviewed you was the consul?"

"'Anything you say will be in strict confidence.' That gave him away. How could anything I said be in strict confidence, when you and the doctor were at the other side of that mirror listening to every word? I imagine you have CCTV for the record."

"What makes you think that?"

"I did teacher training: we had a set up like this for micro-teaching."

"You're paranoid, Brian."

"Paranoid? If I throw this paranoid chair through that paranoid mirror, the lovely doctor and the nauseating pseudo-consul will get a face full of broken glass."

Ralph's face was like thunder. "Well! That's put me in my place."

"And a back-handed compliment for me. He's close to losing it. Jack should goad him into saying what's really on his mind."

Jack was annoyed. "Losing your temper is not going to help. We can either do this in a civilized manner, or I can hand you over to less sympathetic operatives."

"To hell with you and your civilised manner! You're a repulsive leach on the back of humanity, a useless drone with nothing useful to do. You go through life overturning legitimate governments that don't suit your global mission on behalf of the plutocracy."

Maria smiled. "-Now he's talking."

Jack persisted. "Sometimes regime change is desirable."

Brian was furious. "Regime change! Your euphemisms make me want to throw up. What you mean is you kill thousands of innocent civilians to replace dictators who you supported when it suited you."

"How old are you, Brian?"

"You know how old I am; you have my passport."

"It's just that I'm surprised that a man of your mature years can still rattle on like a leftist undergraduate. I was a radical undergraduate once. In the sixties, I abused alcohol and other substances."

"That may explain a few things."

"No call for sarcasm, Brian."

"I suppose you saw the light and were born again?"

"Yes, indeed. I decided to serve my church and my country."

"Very laudable."

"My fellow believers are everywhere, guiding people on the right path."

"They control populations; they teach people to stop thinking about their wretched existence and to look forward to pie in the sky when they die."

"You don't believe there is anything after this?"

"That's the biggest confidence trick of all: if you can con people into believing that, you can con them into believing anything."

In the observation booth, Ralph laughed. "Now who is grilling whom? What do you think, Maria?"

"I think we should call Jack out."

"I'll send a guard. Our guest should go back to his original cell."

"If you insist, Ralph."

Back in Jack's office, Ralph motioned Maria to the armchair and went to stand by the window, which had a view of the mountains to the north of Las Casas.

"This really is a quite beautiful place, Maria."

"Yes, Ralph; it could be another Eden."

"Fat chance, with the rebels at the gates."

Jack came into the office, looked at Maria, lounging in the one comfortable seat and flopped into his office chair. "We need to talk."

"Yes, Jack. Maria and I have come to the conclusion that we're not making much progress."

"No, we're not, and time is pressing. Have you read the reports from last night?"

"Yes, Jack. There was at least one over-flight from the east. What was that in aid of?"

"I think weapons are being dropped into the mountains."

"Why wasn't the plane intercepted?"

Jack patted his paunch. "It was dinner time."

Ralph was appalled. "Great! Everything stops for dinner!"

Maria laughed. "And siesta."

"I'm speechless."

Jack grinned. "Good. Listen. We've had reports of activity in the mountains: weapons training, that sort of thing. I think the guerillas are planning a move.

Ralph was worried. "To another country, I hope. Have you informed the capital?"

"Of course, I have, but there's an election campaign in progress and the army is concentrated in the city."

Maria explained. "Half the population of the country lives in or around the capital, Ralph. Things can turn nasty during elections."

"I don't know why they bother when we all know the result in advance."

"It is what we call democracy."

"I love that word, Jack: it is so loaded with meaning. You have an election: both sides try to stuff the boxes, bribe and intimidate the voters. When the result is declared, the losers cry foul. The problem is that countries that don't play cricket have no conception of fair play."

"This is no time for stupid jokes. Our problem is that we can't expect many troops to be moved down here. Agree, Maria?"

"Yes. It will take at least a week for some to start arriving: we'll get a few raw recruits who will defect to the guerillas rather than get killed."

Ralph gazed out of the window and muttered, "An understandable attitude.

Jack was annoyed. "You've got to realize that we are in a vulnerable position: if the guerillas move on the town in any numbers, we will be helpless."

"Why would they do that?"

"Public relations. Their leader is an intelligent, educated man who wants to raise the profile of his organization. They may stay long enough for the press and TV to arrive, set out their demands and then decamp back to their mountain lair."

"And what are their demands, Jack?"

"They're all about land. They want the big estates broken up and the land given to the Indians."

Ralph scratched his head. "Didn't the neighbour to the south try that in the forties?"

"That government didn't last long; unfortunately we're still mopping up."

"I saw the bodies on the roadside the last time I was down there. What else do the guerillas want?"

"Apparently, their leader wants talks with the government."

"So he has political ambitions."

"Yes. I don't imagine he wants to spend his life on the run in the mountains."

"But if the guerillas are going to come down like wolves on the fold, what are we going to do?"

Jack thought for a moment. "We have to work on our guest. He's fresh from a two-week trip into the mountains. I'm convinced he knows the location of the guerilla bases, their strength and perhaps their plans. If we can't break him soon, we will have to take him to the capital."

Ralph objected. "That will mean risking a road trip through the mountains to the airport at Tuxtla."

"It's only a few hours. We'll be tourists travelling in a camper."

Maria smiled at Ralph. "The rebels won't touch you, Ralph. They don't kidnap tourists. They know it would be bad P.R.

"That's a comfort. Who takes the next turn?"

"Maria will do it. She should go through his record while you observe. You know his CV, Ralph. Try to spot any inconsistencies in his answers; I'll work on them in the following session."

Maria went to the kitchens and collected a plate of rice and meat. She went down the stone steps to the underground cells and looked through the observation grill. The single bulb threw a bright light on Brian who was crouched against the wall and appeared to be watching a line of ants crossing the concrete floor carrying a moth. The walls of the cell ran with moisture and the brown stains bore witness to terrible punishments meted out in the past. She went into the cell and said brightly, "Lunch is served."

Brian was in no mood for jollity. "What's with the downgrading of my accommodation?"

"It must be something you said. Privileges must be earned, Brian; you really should be more polite and not make personal comments. I guess you don't like this cell."

"I can't complain. It's not as bad as Indochina, although this food is just as putrid. At least, I don't risk getting blown up."

"I wouldn't be so sure about that, if I were you."

"Is that so? Are you a real medical doctor?"

"Yes. Five years for my MD and another two for my specialization."

"Why do you collaborate with these morons?"

"There you go again, getting personal. The people who work here are not morons: they are highly intelligent and have the best interests of the country at heart. My job is to take care of the staff and the inmates."

"That must keep you busy: repairing the damage inflicted on them."

"As a rule, the interrogators don't employ crude methods."

"Like torture?"

"Rarely, and against my advice: we haven't lost a prisoner since I arrived."

"Withholding food and water and depriving the prisoners of sleep isn't torture?"

"It depends on your point of view. Americans, like Jack, consider it a legitimate interrogation tactic. I believe it works and the damage done is not usually permanent."

"That's a comforting thought."

Brian was silent for a moment. "As the prisoner said when they strapped him into the electric chair: this will teach me a lesson."

"What lesson, Brian?"

"To do my collecting in less dangerous countries."

"Brian, I can't believe you are scared; you were in Indochina."

"Yes, I was, and I was scared shitless most of the time."

6 Tonkin

Brian had just arrived in Haiphong when his company was dispatched to the south of the delta. It was the first time he or any of his comrades had been in a battle: their first foray lasted forty-five days and they lost eighteen men. Their worst experience happened when they attacked a fortified village; an informer had reported that the village was being used by Vietminh regulars. Brian's company was advancing across the flooded paddy fields towards the village when mortars started to rain down; Brian and Gunter dropped into the mud. Gunter was the first to speak. "Keep your head down."

"If I keep my head any further down, I'll drown in this filthy water."

"This will teach you a lesson."

"What lesson?"

"Not to hit your father with a shovel."

The pair lay prone in the mud, their helmets abutting a dike that divided two paddy fields. The rattle of a machine gun started; they knew that they could not move. Brian tried to drive away his fear with talk. "-You know, Gunter, I think my father was illiterate; at least I never saw him reading."

"How did he manage that?"

"His family had barges: he spent his early years on the canals and hardly went to school."

Gunter was aware that he and Brian were keeping panic at bay with talk. "Did that worry him?"

"I've no idea. I know he resented me reading. If he saw me with a book, he told me to do some work. Get into the field! Do some weeding! Clean the animals out! Do this! Do that!"

"It sounds like the plot from *Le Grand Meaulnes*."

"I've read that: it was one of my French course books."

"You must be an exception; I haven't met an Englishman who spoke another language. We Germans have always been better at learning languages than you English."

"I can't argue with that; our mission is to teach every other nationality English. Once I was reading a newspaper and he shot the back of my hand with an air gun; I bled like hell."

"Was he sorry?"

"I've no idea; he didn't say a word."

"Strange family: what about the rest of them?"

"My grandfather had a Model Lodging House and Restaurant; it was in the street leading to the church. He had six sons and two daughters. The family seemed to have an instinct for survival: all six sons, including my father, joined up in 1914 and went through four years of the war."

"And …"

"They all survived."

"Unbelievable."

"I'd swear my grandfather had made a pact with the Devil."

"Let's hope it's still in force. It's nice lying here in the mud chatting, but what are we going to do now?"

Brian peered over the bank. "Orders are to proceed to that village and weed out the Vietminh."

"According to the sergeant, Vandenberghe was ordered to go in first, open the gates for us and cut a few throats. The sergeant said there wouldn't be any resistance."

"That's why they are raking this paddy with machine guns."

"So, what do we do?"

"We can either stand up and slow march towards the enemy like brave

65

Legionnaires and die or we can crawl in the mud like true cowards."

"You've convinced me. Let's crawl."

Brian was about to crawl onto the dike, when the firing stopped.

"So Vandenberghe and his cut-throats have arrived at last."

A piercing scream rang out. Gunter laughed. "Judging by the screams, he is having fun with his prisoners."

Brian was appalled. "He's a psychopath. Let's go in. Perhaps we can save a few of the prisoners."

"No. Let's stay here for a while. When the butcher is torturing and killing he goes crazy; he's just as likely to shoot us if we catch him at his work."

Brian was surprised. "You seem to know him well."

"I've been on a few of his raids. He's totally fearless; he and his Viets go off at dusk, dressed in black shorts and shirt with only a sausage of rice and their weapons, moving in single file along the dikes. He always has good intelligence: he employs children to go into the Vietminh villages; they laugh and joke with the communists and shout, 'Long live Ho Chi Minh'. Nobody suspects they're spies; they memorize the layout, the defences, the weak spots and numbers and report back to Vandenberghe. He and his killers then move in and do their work. Look! Two Viets are running away from the village."

"Two girls: what are you doing?"

Gunter calmly raised his rifle and got off two shots in quick succession: the children collapsed like rag dolls.

Brian was horrified. "You've killed them! Why? They weren't Vietminh; they were two village children."

"Well, they're dead now."

"What's wrong with you? You enjoyed killing them: you had a horrible smile on your face."

"The heat of battle. Forget it. Let's go and see what Vandenberghe is doing."

Brian would not let go. "Why did you kill those girls?"

"Population control: they'll never produce any little communists."

"That's disgusting."

"Don't just lie there: let's go!"

"You know, Gunter, I'm beginning to think you have developed a taste for killing."

"I'm no different from what I have always been."

7 Paris

Monette, the widow of General de Lattre was at home in her Paris apartment when she had a visit from her friend and confidante, Lilia

"It's so nice of you to come, Lilia. I've been a little depressed."

"Is it the news from Geneva?"

"Yes. They have agreed to Vietnamese independence. It brought memories flooding back. I miss Jean and most of all I miss my son."

"It's only three years since Bernard was killed; you lost Jean only two years ago: you are still grieving."

"I was thinking about Bernard when he was a boy. He was so brave: when the Vichy government put Jean in prison: Bernard, who was only fourteen, helped him to escape. We were allowed visits; Bernard smuggled ropes to his father, hidden in his schoolbag. I delivered a file in a bunch of flowers."

"You were both very brave. But a file is usually in a cake, you know."

Monette laughed. "You are always a tonic, Lilia."

"Bernard was a lovely boy. I have never understood why Jean didn't keep him safe on his headquarters staff. He was Commander in Chief of the French forces and Civil Governor; he had all the powers: he could have saved Bernard."

"Jean wouldn't consider it. Emperor Bao Dai was very fond of Bernard and wanted to have him in his military cabinet; Jean refused his permission, he said when someone bears the name of De Lattre, his place is in the heat of battle."

"In other words, Bernard was meant to die for his country."

"It was inevitable."

"That's something I shall never understand, Monette; this macho man business is rather foolish. I believe in self-preservation and taking care of my own. Reckless bravery is foolishness. I'm surprised that the Army isn't still going into battle on horseback."

Monette was sad. "Now that I am living with the results of Jean's idea of honour, I tend to agree with you."

"I remember that holiday we had in Bao Dai's Dalat palace; you, Jean and Bernard were together for once."

"We had a lovely time but I didn't like Bao Dai. After growing up in France, he was completely unsuited to his position. He was totally out of place at a court thousands of years old with all its ancient traditions and costumes. He was more at home on the Riviera, wearing Gucci, chasing girls and wasting his time and money in the casinos. He never took the position of Emperor seriously; but I was grateful to him during that holiday. He took Bernard hunting in the forest the day before he went back to the delta, and he had a very enjoyable time. I think Jean had a premonition; he asked me to see Bernard off at the airport: it was the last time I saw him alive."

"So Jean thought his son would be killed?"

"Yes. Bernard was sent to the most dangerous part of the defensive line with only Viet soldiers in his company."

"What a waste of a young life. At least Bao Dai tried to save him."

"He did, but he wasn't much use to his country: he refused to live in Hanoi or Saigon, he insisted on sitting out the war in Dalat; what good did he do there? He was a reluctant monarch. After he abdicated in 1945, he went to live in Hong

Kong. He was short of funds and only agreed to go back to Vietnam because he didn't have the money to pay for his gambling and girls. Jean gave him his full backing, but when he tried to put Vietnamese in charge of the government, the Emperor withdrew his support. Jean was furious with him. Bao Dai let him down as did all the other Viets. I wonder what the Emperor will do now his country is independent."

Lilia helped herself to more coffee. "The same as he has always done: keep out of the way and amuse himself. I don't think he ever believed that the monarchy would survive in Vietnam. He extracted the maximum amount of money and privileges and did nothing in exchange. And they are still fighting, Monette."

"Vietnam may now be independent, but the Vietminh still have to show that they are the masters; Giap and his communists are attacking Dien Bien Phu and they won't stop until the French army capitulates."

"Will that happen?"

"It's inevitable. Putting a huge base near the Laotian border was a mistake: the Vietminh have surrounded it and we can only re-supply out troops by parachute drops."

"Those poor soldiers: their losses must be enormous."

"They are being systematically slaughtered. I don't know what our generals were thinking about: common sense argued against the plan."

"Since when did common sense play a part in war, Monette? Will Laos and Cambodia fall?"

"The Americans think so. But I believe the Vietnamese will be satisfied with their independence. Ho Chi Minh has never said he wanted to spread communism."

"The Vietnamese must be sick of fighting."

"And so am I. When I think about our lives, we seem to have staggered from one disaster to another. The first war removed a whole generation from the nation. The economic depression that followed sapped our will; it's no surprise that when the second war broke out, we threw up our hands and said, 'Enough!' No sooner was that lot over than we were into a colonial war."

"You *are* depressed, Monette. Get your coat and hat; I'm taking you out for lunch."

They chose a small restaurant in Montmartre.

"Thank you for inviting me to lunch, Lilia. The food is very good here."

"Not like our Hanoi fare. Why did we eat so badly, in those days?"

Monette perused the menu. "-It was le Roi Jean's decision: he wanted to live simply, not like the Hanoi rich. Our cook complained bitterly: how could such an important man eat such humble fare? He was ashamed of the dishes he had to place on the table."

"I was glad to eat out; I was especially glad when Paul Guinet invited me to one of his dinners. They were splendid affairs; the food was fantastic."

"Jean didn't approve of Guinet and the money men. His soldiers were dying and the war profiteers were making fortunes."

"He wasn't like that in Europe."

"No. In Europe, he had lived like a king at his headquarters, serving up sumptuous banquets for his victorious allies."

"That wasn't the only way he changed; he became much harder, even cruel, in Indochina."

Monette was thoughtful. "And I sometimes doubted his judgment; he associated with people he would have shunned in the past. There was that monster, Vandenberghe. Jean thought he was wonderful but he was a sadistic beast: he organized and trained a band of murderers; they were all Viets he selected from the prisoners; he could recognise which ones would think lightly about torturing and murdering their own people. They used to go into villages and slaughter the Viets; sometimes they massacred the whole village. Jean said with a hundred men like Vandenberghe he could win the war; it was Vandenberghe who brought Bernard's body back to Hanoi. He attacked the ridge where Bernard's post was, and rooted out the Vietminh; he found my son's body. Help arrived four hours later; so much for my husband's master plan. The following July 14th Vandenberghe led the parade; not long after, he was murdered by his own men."

Lilia nodded. "He who lives by the sword …."

8 Dien Bien Phu

The French base at Dien Bien Phu was set in a bowl surrounded by high ground: the French had built their own prison. Brian and Gunter were in a firing point, waiting for Vietminh fighters to appear. None did, but an intermittent barrage dropped mortars on the defences.

Gunter looked at Brian, "Are you all right?"

"What a stupid question! I'm thinking about Frank. Why did you shoot him?"

"I shot him because he was about to shoot you. You should thank me."

"He really hated me. Why?"

"Because he was SS. He hated the British and every other nationality that wasn't tall, blond and Aryan."

"What a load of rubbish that was."

"Not to him. You are dark, and therefore of an inferior race. He didn't see why he shouldn't sodomize you if he wished to."

"Before we jumped, I saw him staring at me and patting his rifle."

"I saw that too: he had a mad look in his eyes. When we went out of the door he followed you; I made sure I followed him."

"I'm glad you did. When I hit the ground, I saw him land, stand up and aim his rifle at me: I thought there must be a Viet behind me. Then he was knocked over."

Gunter laughed. "Though I say it myself, it was a brilliant shot; I hit the ground, rolled over, saw what he was about to do, and shot him. If I'd missed, you would be dead."

The explosions increased in intensity.

"Judging by this artillery barrage, we have only put off our demise for a short time. How did they bring the big guns up?"

"The Viets dragged them up. You know, Brian, I'm beginning to think you and I could run this war better than Navarre."

"We couldn't do any worse. We're sitting in a bowl with Giap's army all around us. What the hell was Navarre thinking about?"

"That the camp would stop the Vietminh from taking Laos; Dien Bien Phu is so remote that they wouldn't be able to get here in any numbers. We arrived by parachute, all our gear came in by plane, but what did they do?"

"They built a road; thousands of Viets with pickaxes and little baskets did the job."

"And our heads are on the block: rats in trap. Joyeux Noel."

"Did you get your Christmas present from the Legion?"

"A packet of cigarettes: not the traditional box of cigars."

"That really pisses me off; I'm used to getting the cigars: I exchanged mine for a watch last Christmas."

A mortar exploded near them. Gunter raised his head. "That was close."

Brian groaned. "Too close. There's something wrong with my leg."

"Let me see."

Gunter cut the trouser leg and opened it. His head went back at what he saw. "I'll get a doctor."

Gunter crawled out of the firing point and ran to the first aid post. Ten minutes later, he dropped into the firing point followed by a Viet girl. Mortars were still exploding nearby.

"No doctor available; there are dead, dying and wounded everywhere. I've brought you a nurse: it's Dong from the brothel."

"I don't need that particular service at the moment."

"She's a very good nurse."

"I suppose she's accustomed to providing relief to the suffering."

"You said it. She'll dress your leg."

"I can see the bone sticking out. I need a doctor."

Gunter nodded to the nurse. "She'll give you morphine to ease the shock."

Brian fell back, exhausted. "Go ahead Dong. You're giving the injection for a change."

9 Las Casas

Brian was in the interview room, staring at the mirror. Jack came in and banged a file down on the table.

"I have your file here. It goes back to your early days; you were a bright boy at school: why did you run away to join the Legion?"

"I felt like a change: that part of Britain is quite depressing."

"A wasteland: mass unemployment; drug addiction; crime."

"That's happened since the miners' strike; it used to be a vibrant community: everybody worked and the lads had their sports clubs. Five and a half days of hard work were followed by football or cricket at the weekend; they had neither the time nor the energy to get into mischief: now the pits have all closed."

Jack smiled. "And the devil has found work for idle hands. The miners were badly led, Brian. They should not have taken the bait and gone on strike. They should have remembered what happened in twenty-six. You know, one of their leaders had a close relationship with a security organization."

"I know about him and his Special Branch connection. Fortunately the man is dead."

"You're pleased about that?"

Brian yawned. "It comes to us all sooner or later."

"But sooner to some."

Brian sat up. "Is that a threat?"

"Yes, Brian. In this part of the world, life is cheap."

"I have noticed."

Jack consulted the file. "When you came out of the Legion, you stayed in France to continue your studies."

"I had the necessary qualifications."

"You were active in the student movement and you often took part in demonstrations: quite the little radical, weren't you?"

"Only when it served a useful purpose."

"A trade unionist was your sponsor: he was a communist."

"According to your definition, he was."

What do you mean by that?

Brian leaned forward. "Anyone who disagrees with you must be a communist."

"Are you a communist, Brian?"

"That's my business."

"You went on a student delegation to the Soviet Union. We started to tag you from that point: that's why your file is so thick. Did you enjoy the trip?"

"It was very interesting."

"We believe the Russians recruited you."

"That's nonsense."

"Your sponsor got you onto a university course."

Brian was getting exasperated. "I've already told you I had the necessary qualifications."

"French, German and English at the British Advanced Level. Is that any good?"

"It's about two years ahead of anything you achieve at eighteen."

"Maybe so, but we get there in the end."

"You had a steady girlfriend in France."

Brian did not answer. Even after many years the pain aroused by that simple statement caused his head to droop. In the mouth of this fascist bastard, it was like a dagger straight into his chest.

10 Hanoi

When Sylvie came into the ward, all heads turned: she was wearing a cheongsam and looked very desirable. Brian was sitting on his bed: he stood up and hobbled, with the aid of crutches, to meet her.

"Hi! As you can see, I am mobile and ready for anything. Let's go to the dayroom: we can talk there."

In the dayroom, they settled into rattan armchairs under a fan. On cue, two Viet servants came in, one with an ice-bucket containing a bottle of champagne; the other with a tray on which were two flutes and a platter of biscuits. The bottle was opened and they toasted Brian's new-found freedom.

"It seems an age since I arrived in Indochina, Sylvie."

"When did you arrive?"

"The same year as De Lattre."

"That was a good year. My brother-in-law, Paul, knew the French wouldn't let Indochina go without a fight."

"How long has Paul been here?"

"Over thirty years. After the second war there was panic when the Japanese assumed control of Hanoi for a while. He borrowed as much as he could and bought hotels and villas from the French who ran away. He got palaces for peanuts. You should see where he lives: all classical pillars and wide terraces. It's beautiful. The Japanese soon departed. The war went badly and Paul added to his investments. Then De Lattre arrived and he started to push back the Vietminh. Things got back to normal, prices rocketed, but Paul knew that it was only a matter of time before Indochina would be lost. He gradually sold off his properties and banked the profits in Singapore and Hong Kong. He'll leave here with a huge fortune."

Brian looked into Sylvie's eyes. "Lucky man."

"No, not lucky: he's very clever; he knows when to bet and when to hold. He's the only racehorse owner in Asia who makes a pile from gambling. He only bets when a race is fixed and he knows the result."

"He prospered and De Lattre died."

"That was very sad. His son, Bernard, was killed in '51 and he died seven months later. He was a great man."

"I think he was a stupid man. A few weeks after we arrived, we spent months working on a wall complete with concrete blockhouses. It was meant to stop the Vietminh from attacking Hanoi and Haiphong but we left a huge gap in the south."

"The wall didn't keep the guerillas out but it did wonders for the price of cement: Paul made millions."

"I sometimes think that our leaders never learn the lessons of history; De Lattre had first-hand experience of the Maginot and Siegfried Lines: they were less use than the Great Wall of China. He still went ahead with his Great Wall of Indochina. It got his son killed; there was a gap in the south, they called it the hole. They couldn't build there because the ground was a swamp. Bernard was on a ridge in the hole when his position was over-run: his Viet soldiers ran away and he was killed."

"Simple minds devise simple solutions: if you want to keep someone out, build a wall. Armies have been doing it since the dawn of history."

"And I finished up in Dien Bien Phu. Building a base there was a brilliant move, I must say: it was a rat trap and we were the rats."

"We were told it was a trap for the Vietminh."

"You have seen how wrong that was; our soldiers are dying in their hundreds; the place is full of wounded with no chance of getting proper treatment: it's a total disaster. The Vietminh are unstoppable; their tactics are horrendous: they attack in force; the first wave is always made up of Viets with Bangalore pipes: they are considered expendable human bombs who blow up fortifications. The regular communist troops follow, en masse, and pour through the breaches: their losses are huge, but so are ours."

"I wish it were all over."

"It will be, but don't hold your breath: it's going to be a long haul, if not for us, for the Americans."

Sophie picked up her bag. "I almost forgot that I have books for you: some San-Antonio stories and a good novel."

Brian looked at a slim novel. "Thanks. *Un Barrage Contre le Pacifique.* This won't take too long."

"The title in the English translation is *The Sea Wall:* the French is better. It's by Marguerite Duras: she's a very good writer but her books are usually short. She was born near here in a Hanoi suburb."

"What's it about?"

"It's a warning to be careful when dealing with the locals. Her poor mother was sold land in Cambodia. She intended to grow rice, the only problem was that the sea invaded the land every year and ruined the crop. She tried to build a sea wall, but it was useless."

"Thanks for telling me the story. After crawling in rice paddies for years, I shudder when I see a bowl of rice."

"Well, you'll have to eat rice every day here."

"Don't I know it. Before I joined the Legion, the only rice I ate was in a pudding with sugar and milk."

"How disgusting! You English don't know how to eat."

"We're learning fast."

"You know, Brian, you were lucky; you came in on one of the last flights out of Dien Bien Phu."

"I know that. When I was hit, there were no doctors free; a nurse dressed my leg."

"There is only one nurse in Dien Bien Phu: that's Genevieve Galand."

"The Angel of Dien Bien Phu, but you are wrong: there are a lot of nurses. They are the girls from the military brothel and they are very good too."

"I hope your nurse took good care of you.
-She did her best. She said if I was good, she would get into bed with me on cold nights but it was never cold."

"A girl after my own heart."

"When a doctor got round to seeing me, he took one look and said he would have to amputate if I stayed there. He managed to get me onto a plane."

"So you still have your leg."

"I do, but I doubt I could get it over."

"I don't understand."

"Never mind."

Suddenly the ambient noise in the hospital grew louder. Sylvie went to the door of the ward, talked to a nurse and came back: her face was serious.

"They're saying that Dien Bien Phu has fallen."

"Oh God! I wonder what has happened to Gunter."

"Your friend?"

"Yes. He was with me when I was hit."

"The rumours coming out are horrendous.

-I can imagine how the Vietminh are treating their prisoners: they have had many years to acquire a thirst for revenge."

"They have also been brutalized by the war: killing, maiming and torturing are second nature to them."

A week later, Brian was given permission to attend Paul Guinet's farewell party as Sylvie's guest. They were greeted by the host.

"Good evening, Sylvie; I see you have found yourself a handsome, young Legionnaire."

"Hello, Paul. This is Brian; he was one of my patients."

"You seem to have done your work well. How are you Brian?"

"Fine, thanks; I threw away my crutches yesterday. This is a wonderful house."

"Yes, indeed. But we are leaving; all civilians have to leave by July the ninth."

"Will you go back to France?"

Paul laughed. "Never. I have bought a hotel in Singapore; the thought of living in France fills me with horror. After thirty year in Asia, enjoying its obvious delights, I could never settle into a bourgeois existence. Here I live; there I would exist. Look at my villa; I could never have this in France. Look at all the servants taking care of my guests; I could never have so many in France. Look at the buffet: how many people in France could afford that?"

"Don't you mind leaving your home?"

"Of course I do, but it's no use crying over spilt milk and I only rent it: I sold it to a Chinese two years ago. Please excuse me; I must go and talk to the General. Have a pleasant evening."

Brian watched Paul waddle away. "He is right about the buffet, Sylvie: I've never seen such a spread."

-The best of imported food. Paul has cleared out his larder: caviar from the Caspian; charcuterie from Lyon; beef, poultry, game from Paris; the choice vintages from his cellar."

"The silver, crockery and glassware must be worth a fortune. If Paul is leaving, what's going to happen to all this?"

"As soon as this farewell party is over, an army of Viets will wash and pack the lot into crates. Everything including the furniture and paintings will go into containers bound for Singapore. Paul is a great planner and he never wastes anything."

Brian glanced around the room. "All the bigwigs from the government are here: all the top brass from the army is here. Why am I here?"

"Because they are old, fat and ugly and you are young, slim and handsome. Can you imagine sleeping with any of them?"

"I can't. Can you?"

"Only if my life depended on it."

Paul came back to them.

"Hello, Paul, I think you have bad news."

"I have to tell you; details are coming in about the retreat from Dien Bien Phu: the Vietminh are marching a huge column of prisoners to the north; I'm told hundreds are dying on the road."

"I hope Gunter makes it; I feel guilty about being here eating and drinking while he is fighting to survive."

"Don't worry; if he's young and single, he'll survive; it's the married men who perish: they aren't as strong as the single men; they worry too much."

Sylvie smiled. "You are a married man, Paul; you would survive; nothing worries you.

"Quite right, Sylvie. I'm a French peasant from generations of peasant stock; I would rather lose a wife than a cow: after all, a cow costs money, a wife comes free. When are you due to quit the Legion, Brian?"

"My time is up. I've done my five years but I don't want to go back to Europe; I'm thinking of signing off here."

"But you won't stay in Hanoi; only the hopeless cases: opium smokers and those who have Viet mistresses will stay."

"I want to visit Singapore and Hong Kong while I decide what to do."

"Call and see me at my hotel in Singapore: it's the Prince Hotel on Orchard Road; you'll enjoy my nightclub."

"Be warned, Brian: don't let Paul fix you up with one of his cast-offs."

"Now, Sylvie, you are misbehaving again: I'm a respectable married man."

"That's new: the only thing you can't resist is temptation."

"Quite right. I'll see you two later. I must go and talk to my guests."

Sylvie watched Paul approach a group in evening dress. "They're from the American Embassy. Paul seems to be getting very close to our American allies."

"I'm not surprised; they are, after all, financing the war. If de Lattre hadn't persuaded them to support France, we would have been out of here long ago."

"And Paul would not be quite so rich. He's an old goat, you know; he usually has a bit on the side."

"Does your sister know?"

"Of course she does. But jealousy is beneath her and she has the best of everything."

"Except for a faithful husband. Will you be going to Singapore?"

"Yes. I'm going to work for Paul. You must come too, Brian."

"I'll think about it. Will you like working in a nightclub?"

"Yes. I must keep up my reputation as an empty-headed, good time girl."

"But you're not empty-headed."

"When a woman lives in Asia, it's better to pretend to be stupid: men expect it. I'll let you into a secret; I have an Arts degree from the Sorbonne: I could teach in a lycee if I chose to."

"Then choose to."

"I'll think about it."

"Surely teaching is better than being a hostess."

"I've no idea. I haven't done either yet; I've been too busy having a good time."

"You'll settle down some time."

"What? When I am old and grey? I can't wait for that."

11 Paris

Monette was thinking about her dead husband and son when Lilia arrived. A maid brought coffee and petits fours.

"Well, Monette, it's all over."

"I heard the news on the radio. The Geneva Accords on Indochina have been signed; all our efforts, all our sacrifices were for nothing."

"Isn't that true of most wars? Why did we try to stay in Indochina?"

Monette took a biscuit, nibbled on it and put it distractedly back on her plate.

"I really don't know. The French people hadn't the slightest interest in it. I remember Jean explaining the official reason: if Vietnam fell, Laos and Cambodia would follow."

"Would that matter? Laos is insignificant. Cambodia is ruled by a mediaeval monarch; they say he has children by two of his aunts."

"Always one for scandalous tidbits, weren't you Lilia?"

"What else is there of interest in this boring life?"

"You should do charitable work; you are a fine nurse. I remember how poor General

Beaufre had his heart attack when we were about to fly to Saigon from Dalat. Le Roi Jean was in a hurry as usual; he wanted to leave him on the tarmac. You took care of him; you persuaded Jean to take him on the plane."

"I believe I saved his life and he is still healthy, living with his wife and many children. Your husband never had any time for the fallen."

"That's true: he could be cruel."

"Jean may be dead, but the Indochina war is still very much alive."

"You mean the Americans? They are taking over where we are leaving off: the last five years of the war haven't cost us a centime; the Americans paid for it and we made a nice profit. Towards the end, they despised us for losing: they saw themselves beating the communists without the help of the effete French or any other country. They really believed that South East Asia would fall to the communists if they didn't lead a crusade against the communists."

"A crusade?"

"Yes, a crusade: they are the most religious people in the world. Urged on by their fundamentalist pastors, they are willing to make any sacrifice to propagate their idea of a free society."

"Religion is fine so long as you don't take it seriously."

"Armies always invoke their God; the German tanks that swept through France bore a cross on their flanks; Jean and the Free French had the Cross of Lorraine. The Americans are different: they really believe they are doing God's work by killing communists."

"They must realize that you can't invade a country and expect to be welcomed by the people. Nationalism is always stronger than any faith. Don't the Americans learn anything from history?"

"History is a closed book for them; so is the map of the world. When Jean came back from Washington, he was very pleased; he had the promise of full American support: lots of dollars, helicopters, tanks, trucks, planes: all the machinery of an industrial war. But what shocked him was the Americans' ignorance of geography; a surprising number had no idea where Indochina was. The ones who did know a little geography could only see China and Mao's millions on the border."

"They learned where Korea was to their cost."

"They stopped the communists in Korea, but finished up accepting partition of the country. They think they can do better in Vietnam, but they won't; they industrialize war: they destroy everything from fifteen thousand feet with more and bigger bombs. You can't win over a country like that, you can only kill the people."

"According to the Geneva agreement, Vietnam has been divided into North and South like Korea."

"That may be so, but the war isn't going to stop: Ho Chi Minh will fight on until the country is reunited. The French were in Vietnam for almost a hundred years; our culture, our food and wine, and our language were well implanted, but we were unable to hold on to the colony. The Americans, with their fundamentalism, coca cola and hamburgers don't stand a chance. The Vietnamese will never give in; they want their country back; they'll fight to the last man, woman and child: our army found that out to its cost."

"Your husband was a hard man, Monette."

"You must understand, Lilia, he was a career military man; he survived the Great War and a serious wound; he won a Croix de Guerre and seven mentions in dispatches; he was wounded again in the 1921 Rif Campaign in Morocco. In 1939, he was the youngest general in the army: after he escaped from Vichy France, he eventually led the 11th army in Europe. You don't lead by being soft."

"But he should never have gone to Indochina."

"No. But he couldn't refuse. Everyone called him le Roi Jean, and he lived up to the name. When he arrived in Hanoi, the Expeditionary Force was in full retreat; he still insisted on parading the exhausted troops whose only thought was to get some rest. He turned the tide of the war and stopped the Vietminh offensive on Hanoi and Giap's attack on Haiphong; he restored the army's morale. He was particularly glad to have the Legion; they were wonderful, loyal fighters. He didn't trust the Viets, but he recruited them in their thousands."

"And all the time he was sick."

"Everybody knew it, but we all pretended that there was nothing wrong with him. Jean thought admitting that he was in pain would be a sign of weakness. His doctor told him he had cancer and didn't have long to live, but he wanted one more campaign, one more hour of glory: that was le Roi Jean."

Lilia was thoughtful. "-If only he had retired after his victories in the Second War, he wouldn't have experienced the shame of defeat."

Monette was a little shocked at that.

"There was no shame; he did his work well; he held the line for a while: long enough to go to Washington and interest the Americans in the war."

"I remember my American friends criticizing us as colonialists: at the end of the war, they wanted us out of Indochina."

"They changed their tune later when they realized Mao's army was on the border with Indochina; they also had the Korean War on their hands and the communist insurgency in Malaya to think about: that made up their minds; they could imagine hordes of communists overwhelming South East Asia and flooding into America. They decided to support us; Jean got helicopters and planes and masses of war supplies. From that point forward the war didn't cost France a centime: the Americans paid for it. In fact, huge profits were made by our industry and commerce; the war was good for many people."

"But not for the men who were fighting it."

"No, war never is, but it's amazing how little civilians care about their soldiers dying."

"It's a sacrifice civilians are willing to make, and they don't spurn the profits from war. I'm not surprised the Americans jumped in so readily: their industries are prospering."

"There's nothing like a war for boosting business: the arms manufacturers rub their hands and scoop up the cash."

"They destroy cities and the infrastructure and then rebuild them: there's no lack of business in wartime."

"Unfortunately, it's a pattern of behaviour that persists. American big business has developed a taste for the fortunes of war:

it's an addiction they will carry on feeding into the next century. Mark my words, Lilia, it will never be satisfied; their proud boast is that America has never lost a war."

"There is always a first time."

12 Hanoi

Brian and Sylvie were waiting in the Hanoi reception area for returning French prisoners.

"Are you sure Gunter will be in this contingent?"

"You can never be sure of anything where the Vietminh are concerned. The Legion was informed that some of their survivors were about to be released: that's as much as I know."

"What does he look like?"

"Tall, blond and very handsome."

"Interesting; he's the opposite of you: short, dark and ugly."

"Thanks, Sylvie."

"Don't mention it. Is that him, over there: the young man with a stick?"

"No. He's much better looking than that."

"Even more interesting. Can you see the distinguished, middle-aged man with silver hair, waiting at the barrier? That's Charles. His friend, a Legionnaire, was at Dien Bien Phu. He's had no news of him, but Charles won't give up hope. I'm told he comes here every day."

"Look! He's running to the column. He's embracing a young Legionnaire."

"And the guards are giving him a beating; so his friend survived; now that's what I call true love, fidelity and a happy ending."

"I hope they live happily ever after."

"Now don't be cynical, Brian. How do I know Gunter isn't your special friend?"

"I believe I have demonstrated my preference for girls who are no better than they should be and I am genuinely pleased that Charles' friend has returned."

"Is there much of that sort of thing in the Legion?"

"What do you mean by 'that sort of thing'?"

"You know what I mean."

"Well, it happens. I had a hard time when I first joined. I was very young but not stupid. Some of the old hands came on to me; one German was a particular nuisance. When I told him to piss off, he took umbrage and promised to kill me later."

"Did it end there?"

"No, it didn't."

"What did you do?"

"I didn't do anything: Gunter killed him."

"How terrible!"

"He was about to shoot me, so Gunter shot him. It's a long story and I know you love long stories, but I'll tell you later. Look! There's Gunter: the tall, blond legionnaire."

"He's very handsome."

-He's having difficulty walking.

"I know the signs: he has bad feet."

"I hope he isn't too bad."

"No, I walk like that when my shoes start to hurt."

"I had a feeling he would come today. We'll have to wait while our officious Vietminh friends go through their bureaucratic rigmarole. That's one thing about the communists: they are fanatical about paper work. God help the ordinary Vietnamese."

"We'll just have to wait until we know where they will send Gunter."

"I'll go and find out."

He marched purposefully to the reception building.

A few days later, Brian went to see Sylvie.

"Can I come in?"

"Need you ask? How is Gunter?"

"He's had malaria and they are keeping him in hospital for a few days to run some tests and treat his feet. Then he'll join me in the Legion barracks."

"Very good. Did he tell you about the long march north from Dien Bien Phu?"

"He did. All the rumours are true: the Vietminh took their revenge on the prisoners; hundreds died of exhaustion, thirst and hunger; some who couldn't keep up were clubbed to death; some were shot. The final contingent of prisoners arrived yesterday: there were some terrible scenes when wives and family members realized that their loved ones weren't coming home."

"How horrible! I'm pleased we are leaving. I love Hanoi but it won't be the same after the communists take over."

"I have some bad news: we have orders to go to Haiphong after the civilians have left; a ship will take us to Marseilles."

"So you won't be coming with me to Singapore?"

"I can't: the Legion won't release me until we have left Indochina; they need every man to protect the civilians."

"Never mind: there are plenty of fish in the sea."

"Is that why a salty tear is running down your cheek?"

"But you will join me after you are released."

"I have a suggestion: why don't you join me in Paris? I'm going to take a teacher training course so that I can teach English."

"Have you got the entry qualifications?"

"I found out this morning that I have: I got a letter from my mother."

Sylvie was surprised. "You've never mentioned your mother, or your family. You only told me why you left."

"I left under a cloud; I never told my mother where I was or what I was doing: I didn't want some flatfoot coming for me to charge me with attempted murder. It was only after I survived Dien Bien Phu that I wrote to her: I had lots of time to think in the hospital."

"So you found out that you had passed the Bac?"

"It isn't the Bac, but the British equivalent: it qualifies me for university entrance."

"What subjects did you take?"

"English, French and German."

"So that's why your French is so good: I've noticed that your grammar is better than most of the native speakers here."

"That was the system: translation both ways and lots of grammar; I only learned to speak the language after I joined the Legion."

"What about your father?"

"I did him a good turn when I hit him with a shovel."

"I feel a long story coming on and I love long stories."

"When they got my father to hospital, they cleaned him up and stitched his wound; he had concussion and, as a precaution, they took an x-ray: they found he had a shell fragment under his skull; they operated and removed it. The doctors said it could explain his erratic behaviour and violent outbursts."

"That's amazing. How did the shell fragment get into his skull? Did you shoot him?"

"The whole story is here: it's a letter from Herbert, one of my uncles who was in the Great War with my father. The six brothers were horse drivers. Herbert and my father were in charge of a pair of Clydesdales."

"What are they?"

"Huge cart horses. They're something like the French Percherons."

"I've seen Percherons: they are enormous."

"My father and Herbert carted ammunition to the front and bodies to the rear. When the shells started to fall, they walked between the horses. It saved them in nineteen seventeen; a shell burst: my uncle heard the shrapnel thudding into the ribs of the horse on his right. It sank slowly to the mud, taking him and my father with it. Another explosion and the horse on the left dropped."

"Were they badly hurt?"

"The horses?"

"No, stupid: your father and your uncle."

"When Herbert came to, a couple of French soldiers were carving chunks from the dead horses. He tried to stop them, but he couldn't move; he couldn't hear; he couldn't speak; he lay in a trough of horse blood and guts: it was warm so he slept."

"What about your father?"

"My father didn't say a word until he was shipped home. Equipment at the front was basic and they never noticed the shell fragment in his head. The doctors called his condition shellshock, but they couldn't be sure that he wasn't slinging the lead: they treated him like the village idiot. My uncle wasn't much better; he could hardly hear, but he could talk: they let him look after his brother."

"Didn't you know any of this?"

"Not a word; not even my mother knew: I've told you my father was a man of few words. Herbert says his brother used to wander from the hospital into the town. There was a quiet public garden; he used to sit on a bench every afternoon and stare at a fountain: Herbert used to follow him."

"And your father still couldn't communicate? Not even by signs or writing?"

"I don't think he could write. One afternoon Herbert and my father were in the public garden when a woman and a sad little girl with great green eyes arrived; the woman sat on a bench while the little girl played. My father started to eat a bar of chocolate; he noticed the woman watching him, so he gave her the chocolate: she shared it with the little girl."

"So he was aware of what was happening."

"Obviously. Herbert was never quite sure whether some of it wasn't an act to avoid being sent back to the front. The next day my father wandered through the hospital kitchens and filched a tin of bully beef. When he gave it to the woman, she started to weep: it upset him so much that he didn't go to the garden again."

"So he was very sensitive."

"Evidently he was, but he never talked about his wartime experiences. I think they stayed with him longer than he would admit: he sometimes fell asleep in his chair and mumbled; I think he had bad dreams."

"The poor man; is that the end of the story?"

"Not at all."

"Oh, good!"

"A week later, Herbert and my father were wandering in the town when they saw the woman and her child. They were sitting on the steps of their house, warming themselves in the afternoon sun. The woman saw my father and put her hand to her mouth."

"What did he do?"

"He went back to the hospital kitchens; he was the village idiot; nobody ever took any notice of him. When the coast was clear, he filled his haversack with food from the piles in the kitchen: meat, vegetables, butter and bread. He added a bottle of the rough red wine the cooks drank all day long: my father gave the food to the woman. When she said 'Au revoir', he found himself repeating the words. They were the first words he had managed to get out since he was blown up: he decided to keep his mouth shut from then on."

"He didn't want to go back to the front."

"No. My father fed the woman and the little girl for two months. At first, he was careful to only take a little of each food from the kitchen; one day, he got careless and took a whole chicken. Even the drunken cooks noticed; they started to watch the kitchen and he was caught with his hands in a bowl of fresh liver: my uncle says he was caught red-handed."

"I think that is a joke but don't explain it."

"The doctors had another go at him; he heard them say 'hysterical dumbness' and 'kleptomania'. They decided he was a hopeless case and sent him back home; the war was almost over anyway. He never saw the woman and her child again, but the last time he had seen them, they were rosy cheeked and plump."

"So your father went back to England. Was he all right?"

"It took him a few months to get back to normal. The war was over; he was soon in the pub playing darts and chatting with the lads. He got a disability pension for being a maniac, but at the next meeting of the board, they took it away: they said one of their investigators had seen him in the pub behaving normally; one of the regulars had shopped him. He went back to working the barges; eventually he married and bought a small holding."

"But he had a shell fragment in his head: it must have affected him."

"I know he had headaches and occasionally went into a violent rage, but we didn't know why."

"Will you go and see him?"

"I'll think about it."

"You should go. You didn't write for years; your mother didn't know whether you were dead or alive; she must have been worried."

"I suppose she was, but you have to understand, some British families are rather cold with each other."

"The traditional British phlegm."

"That's right. It's a relic of Victorian prudery: showing your emotions is regarded as unseemly."

"What a strange lot you are. Being British isn't a nationality, it's an incurable condition."

"We can visit Gunter tomorrow. Would you like to come?"

The hospital was busy with sick and wounded who had returned from Dien Bien Phu; they found Gunter in the day room.

"Hello, Gunter. This is my friend, Sylvie."

"Thanks for coming, I was really bored."

"We've brought you some magazines."

"Thanks."

"At least you're not in bed."

Gunter winced. "My feet are still bad but they let me spend most of my time in the day room and I eat in the canteen."

"What's wrong with your feet?"

"I wore my boots out on the long march, then my feet got cut to ribbons before I managed to get hold of a dead man's boots."

"But you'll be OK?"

"Sure. I'm healing nicely: I'm better off than most of the survivors."

"We'll be moving out soon."

"I know, Brian."

"What are you going to do when you get back to France?"

Gunter was calm. "I'll sign on for another five."

Sylvie stopped admiring the handsome blond hunk for a moment and interjected, "You do know that there may be war in Algeria."

Gunter raised his hands. "I'm certain there will be a war in Algeria. The Algerians have seen how easily the Vietminh disposed of the French Expeditionary Force."

Brian was dismissive. "French Algeria is a fiction: how can an African country be part of France?"

Gunter was firm. "Ours is not to wonder why. I've got used to the life of a legionnaire; I don't have to think about paying for my keep; I eat and drink well and the girls in the military brothel are charming."

Sylvie intervened. "Algeria is an Islamic country. I don't think you'll find an army brothel there."

"Don't you believe it; I've discovered one constant in life: where there are legionnaires, there are brothels. What are you two going to do? Get married?"

"Perish the thought. Can you imagine anyone marrying this ugly Englishman?"

"Sylvie is going to Singapore to work in her brother-in-law's nightclub and I'm going back to school."

Sylvie was indignant. "Wait a moment, I may not want to marry an ugly Englishman, but I'm thinking of joining him in France."

Brian was overjoyed. "Fantastic! I can't believe this."

"On one condition: you should study in the South, Montpellier, say, the weather down there is much more to my taste; I hate the cold, wet winters in Paris."

"But what will you do?"

"I told you: I'm qualified to teach in a lycee; that's exactly what I will do."

Gunter grinned. "Then you can keep Brian in the style he's accustomed to."

"That won't be difficult; I'll be happy with a loaf of bread, a jug of wine, a well-done steak and chips and thou, Sylvie."

"I can see that I will have to educate your palate: a steak should never be well done."

"Can you cook?"

"Can a fish swim? I'm half French and half Vietnamese. You will have the best of both worlds."

Gunter placed his hands over his heart.

"Isn't love wonderful!"

13 Las Casas

In the interview room, Jack saw at once that he had hit a raw nerve with the mention of Brian's Eurasian girlfriend.

"What's the problem, Brian?"

"You know what the problem is."

"It was a long time ago."

"Can you change the subject?"

"I'm not a monster, Brian: I can understand what it is to lose a child, even if it was only a foetus."

"I'm sure you can".

"So you enjoyed your studies in Montpellier."

"I did."

"Before you started your course, you and your girlfriend went to Paris for a vacation. You met a rising star in the French Communist Party; he welcomed you into his home and introduced you to younger members of the Party; the French Communists were very active."

"The spirit of 1789 and the Communes."

"You and your friend stayed for two months in a room on the Left Bank, long enough to get acquainted with several leading activists. Why didn't you stay in Paris? "

"Sylvie had a post in Marseilles and I had registered for a course at Montpellier."

The door opened and a young man came in with a coffee. Jack beamed.

"Ah. Here's my handsome, young friend, Jose, with our coffee."

As Jose placed the tray on the table, Jack ran his hand down the young man's side.

"Thank you, Jose."

"Be careful, Jack. Your sexual preference is showing."

Jack was furious.

"Watch your mouth. If I choose, I can give you to the guards."

"Go to hell!"

Jack stood up, his chair went over, and his fist flapped the air ineffectually as he tried to hit Brian.

In the observation booth, Maria was alarmed. "Call Jack out, Ralph: he just took a swing at our guest."

Ralph was unfazed. "And he missed."

Jack had calmed down when he came back to the interview room. "Where were we?"

"You were trying to knock my head off."

"It can still be arranged. You studied for the next four years and taught night school. Why?"

"I worked part time at the Berlitz School. I needed the money; what I saved during my time in the Legion did not last long."

"In that time you only visited England once; your family was there; had you no intention of living there?"

"I intended to stay in France. I didn't want to live among the slag heaps."

Jack smiled. "Well, the slag heaps have now been leveled and the pits have gone."

"Even then, the writing was on the wall; oil was going to replace coal."

"The writing was written large before the last strike: the lady finished off the union."

"She was no lady."

"You didn't like her strategy?"

"Her strategy was brilliant; she always intended to close the pits. Her plan worked perfectly."

"So you admire her?"

Brian snorted. "In the same way that I admire Genghis Khan and Attila the Hun."

"I want to ask you about Gunter."

Brian went pale. "-Don't bother."

Jack continued. "You met him again in France and then in Singapore. Did you know who employed him?"

"No. I just have to live with the results of his actions."

4 Palavas-les-Flots

Brian and Sylvie were sitting on the terrace of a café in Palavas-les-Flots, a charming fishing port south of

Montpellier; a cool breeze came in from the sea.

"Are you warm enough, Sylvie?"

"Yes. But I'm glad that I have my fur jacket."

"How did it survive the heat and humidity of Hanoi?"

"-My sister-in-law, Marguerite put it into cold storage with her furs."

"Does she wear furs? She certainly won't need them in Singapore."

"She travels to New York and Milan to buy clothes: she'll need them there."

"Have you heard from her?"

"I got a letter a few days ago: she and Guinet are fine. He had a fright a few weeks ago: he was in a convoy going to Ipoh when it was ambushed by communist terrorists."

"He wasn't hurt?"

"No. But he says he won't be visiting Malaya for a while."

"Singapore seems to be quite safe; the war has hardly affected it."

"They don't call it a war; they say it's an emergency."

"The Brits want to keep the whole thing low key; they can also claim insurance in an emergency but not in a war."

"The communists are still murdering and torturing rubber planters and civilians."

"They aren't so keen on tackling the military except in ambushes; the Brits and Commonwealth troops are gradually getting the upper hand: they're moving civilians into protected areas so that the communists can't get support from them."

"It seems that they are going to do something the French couldn't manage: win a war against the communists."

"How is Paul's business, by the way?"

"As in every war, places of entertainment are thriving; Singapore is a rest and recreation centre for the Americans: Paul's hotel and nightclub are booming; he's a very good businessman."

"What about the dodgy side of the business?"

"He's given up trying to fix horse races but he still provides escorts."

"You mean prostitutes."

"Escorts: prostitute is such an ugly word."

"It's an ugly business."

"Paul interviews lots of girls for his hotel and club; he is not above resorting to the casting couch. Marguerite says she caught him out when she walked in on one of his interviews: the girl was naked."

"Perhaps he wanted to authenticate her attributes."

"The girl was a singer and Paul was naked too."

"It must have been difficult to explain that one away."

"He has the nerve of the devil; he would laugh it off in his usual manner. Have you heard from Gunter?"

"Yes. His company was sent to Constantine to deal with the insurrection: the rebels had murdered a hundred Europeans."

"Did you read what Mitterand said last week? 'Algeria is France and war is the only negotiation we are prepared to take part in'."

"What a stupid attitude; he's a politician and he'll go far. How did school go last week?"

"Very well. I like the students."

"t's a pity you couldn't get a post in Montpellier: we could be together all the time instead of just on occasional weekends and holidays."

"You could come to Marseilles more often."

"I will."

"You know our education system: for a first post, teachers go where they are sent. I've applied for Montpellier but most teachers want Paris, so it shouldn't take long for me to get what I want."

"What do you think of Palavas-les-Flots?" Sylvie took in the picturesque quay and the fishing boats.

"It's beautiful: so un-spoilt and I loved the Little Train from Montpellier."

"It won't last; the most unlikely places are being developed as tourist resorts."

"They will have to solve the mosquito problem."

"They'll drain all the marshes."

"What about the rice paddies?"

"They'll go for golf courses."

"And the Camargue with the beautiful white horses?"

"Hotels and horse meat."

"You are an old cynic."

"I suppose I am. But for you, I would be a manic depressive like my father."

"I thought he was cured."

"Not really: he still has his moments; war does nasty things to people."

"You seem to have come out of Indochina very well."

"When you are in your teens you don't see the dangers. I was quite oblivious to death; it was something regrettable that happened to other people. As I got a little older and wiser, I decided to stop pushing my luck; a certain lady also came into my life."

"And gave you a reason to live."

"Come on; let's throw caution to the winds and have another coffee."

15 Paris

Monette and Lilia were having a celebration dinner in the Tour d'Argent.

The company was lively and there was only one topic of conversation.

"Well, Monette, I thought dinner here would be a suitable way to celebrate de Gaulle's election."

"At last we have a worthy president. If only Jean had lived, he would have been delighted to see his old comrade governing France."

"Perhaps Jean would have been in that position; some people say he had the presidency in mind."

"He never said so; he was a simple soldier, he didn't have the guile to be a politician; but he understood geopolitics: he once said that the world's centre of gravity had moved from Europe to Asia and he was right."

Lilia put down her menu. "Have you chosen?"

"I'll have cuisses de grenouille; the V on my plate will celebrate de Gaulle's victory."

"I'll join you. They are delicious here."

"Everything is delicious here; it's only the bill that gives you indigestion."

They placed their order. Lilia turned to Monette, "Do you think de Gaulle will win the war in Algeria?"

"That's impossible; he is a pragmatic politician: he will work out a compromise with the FLN and Algeria will get its independence."

"I had lunch with General Salan last week; he is firmly against Algerian independence."

"Salan is a dinosaur; I remember the mess he made in Indochina."

"Francois Mitterand agrees with him; so do the Legion and a large part of the General Staff: I think there will be a coup in Algiers."

"It's inevitable; the Legion will join any coup plot; they built Sidi-Bel-Abes: it's their town."

"They won't want to leave it; their war memorial is there."

"That may be so, but if we can bring obelisks from Egypt, we can ship a war memorial from Algeria to France."

"Do you know what I like most about de Gaulle?"

"His dashing good looks?"

"Don't make me laugh; he is a man of principle. When most of our leaders were accepting the armistice with Hitler, he dug his heels in and refused: he went to England to continue the fight."

"He will continue to fight for French independence."

"We are independent."

"Do you think so?"

"We are in thrall to the Americans. De Gaulle dislikes the present international arrangements: he wants France to have her own nuclear deterrent and to take us out of Nato."

"Are you sure about that?"

Monette smiled conspiratorially. "I have it from a very reliable source."

"Why do we dislike the Americans so much?"

"They saved Europe; perhaps we feel guilty about the poor show we put up in

1940. We used to be a proud nation; De Gaulle wants to restore our pride."

"You should go into politics Lilia."

"I'm too old for that."

"You have an American friend, don't you?"

"Yes, but when she is in Paris she says she is Canadian; as you know, we French love Canadians."

"What shall we have now?"

"Lobster and a bottle of Champagne."

"Why not? We'll drink a toast to de Gaulle."

"And to your late husband: two great patriots."

16 Marseille

Brian and Sylvie met Gunter in a Marseille restaurant.

"It's good of you to come; it's so nice to see you both again, and looking so well."

Sylvie smiled. "The life here suits us and I have an interesting job."

"And I am a student; it's a great life. I was surprised when I got your note, Gunter. Why are you in Marseille?"

"There's a new Legion depot near here. It's used a lot for rest and recreation. They're getting ready for the time when we have to leave Algeria."

"Is that likely?"

"It's inevitable; the people hate us. We are using the worst imaginable methods to control them. As far as I can judge, they are willing to die to the last man."

"Indochina all over again. What about Sidi-bel-Abbes?"

"The town the legion built? It will probably become a tourist resort. Now to more important matters; this restaurant is the best on the Cannebiere and it has the best bouillabaisse in France. Would you like that Sylvie?"

"Of course. And Brian will have it too; it's our staple diet when we visit Palavas. We'll see if it is any better in Marseille."

"Are you two going to marry?"

Sylvie shook her head. "Not for the moment. The saying that 'two can live as cheaply as one' is fiction. We live like students and manage nicely. If we set up house, we would notice our shortage of cash; as it is, we don't worry about anything. What about you, Gunter? Are you still intent on a lifetime in the Legion?"

"No. I'm not going back to Algeria; I shall go on leave from here next week to visit my family in Germany and not come back."

"What happened to change your mind?"

"I saw some terrible things in Tonkin; the Vietminh were as bad as the French. We have the same situation in Algeria; car bombs, indiscriminate killing; the rebels torture captured soldiers, then we go into a village and cut the throats of the whole population; prisoners are tortured and then dumped from helicopters into the sea. It's sickening: I don't want any more of it."

Sylvie was concerned. "You'll be a deserter."

"Like thousands more."

Brian added his warning. "You will have a hard time if the Legion catches you."

"If I stay out of France, I won't have a problem."

Sylvie nodded. "I think you are doing the right thing: the Algerian war is a horrible waste of lives."

Brian frowned. "But what about the Pieds Noirs? There are thousands of French settlers and descendants of settlers. What will they do?"

"They will do what the French did in Indochina: leave; there are lots of French territories which welcome them: French Polynesia, New Caledonia, New Hebrides, Guiana and Devil's Island …"

"I suspect you are becoming a radical, Sylvie."

"Of course I am, Gunter. The way things are in the education system is intolerable. One of these days, there's going to be a rebellion, not soon, but sooner or later; mark my words: students and workers will be on the barricades."

"A new Commune."

"Yes. And they won't be able to transport the Communards to New Caledonia, like they did in the past."

Gunter chuckled. "No. New Caledonia is now a very desirable place to live: eternal springtime and an easy life without the disadvantages of having to work too hard: the Legion loves it. Here comes the bouillabaisse."

The waiter ladled out the soup which was tasted and approved. Sylvie delivered her judgment. "Just the right amount of garlic."

Brian agreed. "Better than ours. Thanks, Gunter."

"It's my pleasure."

Sylvie sighed. "If only life was as simple as this: supreme happiness in a fish soup!"

Brian helped himself to more soup. "What will you do in Germany, Gunter?"

"I shall go into business."

Sylvie was curious. "What kind of business?"

"Something interesting, secure and not too demanding: something that will interest an ex-legionnaire."

"Does such a business exist?"

"I don't know. I shall have to find out. "

"What about capital? You may need capital."

"I have a solid account in Hamburg. I dabbled in piastres in Indochina. I worked a scam with an employee at the official bureau de change. We circulated over-valued piastres for francs between Hanoi and Paris; the official needed me to act as the client."

Sylvie smiled. "So you were a nasty war profiteer."

"I was indeed."

"My brother-in-law was the king of the rackets."

"Paul Guinet. I knew him well."

"You did? I never saw you at his dinners."

"Our business was strictly private: socializing was out of the question."

"How mysterious! Well, good luck with your business, whatever it is, Gunter."

17 Singapore

When Brian finished his degree, he and Sylvie decided to take up an offer of a holiday in Singapore, all expenses paid by Paul Guinet. They were sitting by the poolside at the Intercontinental Hotel waiting for Paul to arrive.

Sylvie was happy to be back in the Orient.

"It's lovely here by the pool. The evening is warm. The lights are soft. The scent of satay grilling over charcoal is driving me mad."

"You have developed an obsession for food, especially spicy food, Sylvie."

"Yes, I have. I think it's because I'm pregnant."

"What! Pregnant! How could you be pregnant?"

"Think about it, Brian. What does it take to make a baby? Cat got your tongue? It takes precisely what we have been doing with abandon for the last few years; I'm surprised it has taken this long."

"I don't know what to say."

"Don't say anything. Just think about how you are going to support a wife and child."

"Of course, I'm delighted."

"No, you're not. You're thinking that the good times are over; you can see a black cloud of responsibilities hovering over you."

"You're right, as always. I'll go and ask the woman to bring us some satay while I allow this news to sink in."

"Ask for extra satay sauce and raw onions. Sylvie saw the rotund figure of her brother-in-law approaching. He looked worried and his greeting was far from effusive."

"There you are, Sylvie."

He looked round the pool before taking a chair.

"Paul! What took you so long?"

"It's a long story."

"As everybody knows, I love long stories."

"Where's Brian?"

"Over there, talking to the satay woman. Here he comes."

"Paul! It's so nice to see you again after all this time."

"Nice to see you, Brian. How long is it?

"Over five years."

Sylvie perused Paul's worried face. "What's wrong, Paul? Why are we staying here? And where is my sister?"

"I booked you in here because I am having problems with certain people. I didn't want you involved. I've sent Marguerite and the children back to France: they'll be safe there."

"Why didn't she tell me? Where is she?"

"She's in Paris in our apartment and she didn't tell you because I told her not to."

Brian started to get up from his chair.

"Shall I leave you two to talk?"

"Stay, Brian. I think of you as family."

Paul spoke quietly.

"Do you know your friend Gunter is in Singapore?"

"What's he doing here?"

"He's in a certain business which involves solving problems for a certain powerful government."

Sylvie interrupted. "What does that mean?"

"Among other things, he arranges assassinations; he's a hitman. He enjoys his work and he's good. I can't tell you too much, but I have been involved with certain elements in Vietnam."

"The Americans?"

"I can't say."

"Come off it, Paul. If the situation is that bad, why aren't you in France with your wife and family?"

"I will be, but I have to finalize my business here: I've got a lot invested in Singapore."

"Can't Brian and I represent you?"

"That's why I asked you to come. I can trust you; I have arranged power of attorney for you. I'll give you all the papers relating to my legitimate businesses: everything is here in this briefcase."

"And the not so legitimate enterprises?"

"We'll write them off. Here comes your satay."

"I wish I could say I had lost my appetite, but I haven't. Have some satay, Paul."

"Thanks, but I'm not hungry: you two go ahead."

Brian leant forward and spoke to Paul.

"There's a man at a table over there. He keeps glancing at us."

"He's probably watching me. I can't go back to my hotel; I'm staying here tonight: we can go through the papers in my room. I'm booked on Air France to Paris for tomorrow afternoon."

Sylvie was worried. "Who is that man, Paul?"

"I don't know."

Sylvie noticed Paul had a pistol on his lap.

"What are you doing with that gun, Paul?"

"I'm preparing to welcome a visitor."

"Surely you are safe here, with all these people around."

"I hope so, but you never can tell; we are living in dangerous times."

Brian stood up. "Shall I call security?"

"That might be good idea."

"He's coming this way."

Before Paul could react, the man produced a gun and shot him in the head. Brian heard two thuds from a silenced revolver; the man fell into the pool. Blood started to cloud the water: Sylvie was rigid with fear. "He's shot Paul!"

"Are you all right, Sylvie?"

"Yes, I'm all right. Get a doctor for Paul."

"Look at him. He's dead."

"What about the killer?"

"He's in the pool; judging by the amount of blood in the water, he's dead too."

"Did Paul shoot him?"

"No, he didn't manage to fire a single shot: the shots came from above."

"Look! Up there on that balcony!"

"It's Gunter. What the hell is he doing here? Stay here, Sylvie. I'm going to catch up with our German friend."

Brian ran up the stairs to the first floor of the hotel: Gunter was waiting for him.

"Slow down, Brian: you get nothing in a hurry, except perhaps a baby."

"What are you doing here?"

"I've just eliminated an expendable hitman: a beautiful shot. You see, my time in the Legion was not exactly wasted."

"Why? Why did you let him kill Paul Guinet?"

"I shouldn't answer your question, but, for old times' sake, I will. Paul was a danger to an important organization; he was about to reveal certain information relating to Vietnam; we couldn't let that happen. A Thai gangster will take the blame."

"I trusted you, Gunter."

"You should never trust anyone, Brian."

"I should have known you were a murderer."

"I gave you plenty of evidence of that."

"You killed those Viet girls for fun. What did you do when you went on raids with Vandenberghe?"

"I tortured, mutilated and killed Viets."

"You fascist …"

"At last you have seen the light. You were so naïve; you would swallow any old cock-and-bull story provided it was suitably sentimental."

"What the hell are you?"

"What I have always been: a crusader in the war against communism and liberals like you and Sylvie. Goodbye, Brian.

Don't follow me, otherwise I shall have to shoot you too."

Gunter walked away slowly, keeping Brian in view until he turned a corner. Back at the poolside, the commotion caused by the shooting was at its peak Brian took Sylvie in his arms. She said, "What was Gunter doing here?"

"It's another long story; I'll tell you later. You are very pale; are you all right?"

"I think so. What are we going to do?"

"Take the briefcase and sort out Paul's affairs. Where is it?"

"It's gone: the briefcase has gone; someone has taken it. What are we going to do?"

"We obviously aren't going to finalize Paul's affairs; we'll just have to leave it to the lawyers. Go to bed, Sylvie, you need your rest: I'll go and talk to the police."

"They're all over the place; they aren't Singaporean police; they're Brits. They must have been nearby to get here so quickly; they took Paul's body away and fished the gunman out of the pool."

"It's almost as if they knew what was going to happen."

"That's my impression too."

18 Paris

Lilia was with Monette who had just returned from a trip that had brought back sad memories.

"How was your trip, Monette?"

"Crowded with memories, Lilia. I visited Jean's grave: I felt a surge of pride, seeing him lying next to Clemenceau."

"Two great Auvergnats."

"I also went to Opme to the house where Jean was imprisoned. I could almost see Bernard, fourteen years old, going to visit his father: if only my son had been spared."

"Did you get to Clermont-Ferrand?"

"Yes. I attended the Congress of the First Army; the members were very kind and welcoming, but I knew so few of them."

"Very few soldiers live into old age: the second war, Indochina and Algeria decimated our armed forces."

"I met the President; he was most kind; he told me how much he admired Jean and how sorry he was that I lost my son. He also thanked me for some documents I had passed on to the security services."

"What documents?"

"I can tell you now because there's going to be a huge public scandal."

"Do tell."

"Some time ago, I received a package from Paul Guinet."

"I did so enjoy his dinner parties in Hanoi. How is he, by the way?"

"He's dead: he was assassinated by a Bangkok gangster. It appears the killer was hired by an ex-legionnaire, a deserter, who was involved with the CIA on covert operations."

"He killed people for them?"

"Yes. He wanted cover for the assassination of Guinet, so he hired the gangster; he watched him kill Paul and then shot him. Fortunately an ex-legionnaire, who happened to know Guinet and the German, witnessed the whole incident."

"So why are the documents Guinet sent you so important?"

"They contain details of some highly illegal operations in Vietnam, involving several Washington officials."

"Why did Paul Guinet send the material to you?"

"He was aware that the CIA was going to try to kill him; he trusted me to make sure that the information was not buried by the French government."

"That's hardly likely with our current president; he hates the Americans. So you passed it on our security service."

"Yes. They got in touch with Washington; several prominent officials resigned; one went to the World Bank."

"The World Bank job is the usual reward for failure; so why is the scandal coming out now?"

"The man who witnessed the murder is married to Guinet's sister in law."

"Not the wild one."

"She's calmed down. She was teaching in a lycee in Marseille. Well the witness was in the Legion with the assassin; he gave our secret service details of his activities and where he was living. The man, a German, was arrested and is now serving a life sentence for several murders. Some say, unfortunately, but I say, fortunately, the trial gave the press the details; little by little, the reporters uncovered the whole dirty episode."

"Politicians think they can get away with anything, but they always get caught out in the end."

"One more thing came out in the trial: you remember the Moulin a Vent executions in Lyon, don't you?"

"Yes, it was in 1945. The war was almost over but the Germans shot four prisoners in front of the cafe. There's a memorial there now: *Le Veilleur de Pierre*."

"It transpired at the trial that the German assassin was in the firing squad that executed the Resistance men. He always maintained he wasn't involved but a witness came forward and testified that he was."

"So justice has been done after all these years."

"Yes. And the Americans are furious: their dirty linen is about to be washed in public."

"I have no sympathy with them; they thought they could pacify Vietnam; they wouldn't listen to our people who had so much experience. Will they never learn their lesson?"

"Lilia, there's one lesson you should have learned: our leaders never learn."

19 Las Casas

Jack was grilling Brian about his travels.

"You and your wife were with Paul Guinet when he was killed: how much did you know about him?"

"I knew he had done well out of the Indochina War and that he did business with some shady characters."

"Like who?"

"Like you and your colleagues."

"Is that so? Do you know that we thought about picking you up and sequestrating you in one of our special facilities?"

"Like the one I am in now?"

"Yes. If you disappear, nobody will know a thing."

"Like Jim Thomson in Malaya."

"I can see that you understand me. The fact that you were a close friend of the man who orchestrated Guinet's murder was a sufficient reason to go after you."

"But you didn't. Why?"

"I can't tell you that."

"You don't need to. Gunter was your man and Guinet was in cahoots with your organization. You knew I had nothing to do with Paul Guinet's murder."

"After the murder, you stayed in Singapore for a while."

"My wife miscarried and she was in the hospital."

"And you did not have any more children."

"No. It was a consequence of the miscarriage."

"That must make you very sad."

Brian was annoyed. "Can we change the subject?"

"You and your wife went back to France; she resigned her job and you both stayed with her sister."

-Paul's widow. My wife needed more medical treatment.

"You took a teaching job with Berlitz. Why did you choose them?"

"The students were engineers and salesmen. The school preferred more mature teachers who had some experience of life."

"You lived in France until 1965 and you spent a lot of time with your comrades; you were seen at public meetings and street demonstrations."

"French society was set in aspic. Power and wealth were in the hands of the bourgeoisie. The *status quo* meant that the scions of rich families swamped the *grandes ecoles* and therefore the government and Civil Service. There were rumblings from the younger generation and the Party was trying to channel them into positive action."

Jack applauded slowly. "Nice speech. I guess you have given that a few times. You did a fair amount of travelling when you were in France. You traveled in Central Europe. You had a brief affair with a lady from the Eastern Bloc."

"As you say, it didn't last long."

"You were hardly a faithful husband."

"I don't pretend to be perfect."

"We were very pleased by your little fling. We filed the information under B for Blackmail. She was one of ours, you know, and she gave us a full report. She had you down for a dangerous radical who wouldn't hesitate to take part in terrorist operations."

"I dumped her very quickly and rather unceremoniously: hell hath no fury like a woman scorned."

"She recorded some of your tirades; I tend to agree with her. We stepped up surveillance after that."

"I noticed. That woman should be prosecuted for wasting public money; have you ever worked out how much your lot has spent on dogging my footsteps?"

"We can never spend too much on national security."

"Even when the allegations come from a vengeful woman?"

"Especially when they come from a vengeful woman; is that why you left Europe and went to Singapore?"

"No. I was ready for a change; my wife went to help her sister in their hotel."

"A lot was happening in the region: Vietnam, for example."

"It wasn't going too well for you, was it? The Vietcong were in the Embassy at Tet. You carpet bombed Hanoi on Christmas Day 1972: how's that for Old Testament type revenge?"

"We stopped the dominoes falling."

"That excuse for murdering civilians is getting a little tired."

"You spent a lot of time with the French community."

"My wife was French."

"Eurasian and likely to sympathize with her mother's people."

"Of course. Do you find that un-natural?"

"When you arrived in Singapore, several communists were on the run."

"You mean the ones who won seats in the 65 election?"

"Yes. The ones who refused to take their seats."

"And were either thrown in jail or went on the run."

"The ones who weren't caught got outside help."

"I don't know where from."

"Maybe from you: we think you were a courier."

"Of what?"

"Fake passports, money."

"I'm afraid not."

"It was also the time of the communist coup in Indonesia."

"There was no communist coup; the only coup was the one engineered by your lot to neutralize Soekarno: your hit squads murdered a million Chinese."

"You underestimate, and they were communist terrorists."

"Then you liquidated the hit squads."

"It was a beautiful operation: no loose ends. We got very good PR, the media put out all the propaganda we gave them: according to the historical record, we foiled a communist coup."

"You put your man in, he then proceeded to rob the country blind."

"As a good ally, he deserved the reward for his loyalty. You made friends with a number of British Army officers; every weekend you visited a different military base."

"Singapore was full of bases. I played rugby for a team that always played away."

"The *Tankards*. Why the name?"

"We played away for the free beer in the messes: we drank a lot of beer."

"And you collected a lot of intelligence."

Jack was in his office, feet on his desk, hands clasped over his colonial egg. When Maria and Ralph came in, he sat up. Maria smiled.

"Our guest is back in the VIP cell."

Jack was not pleased. "Is that a good idea?"

"He's being a good boy. He'll believe he's being rewarded."

"What do you think, Ralph?"

"So far he hasn't put a foot wrong. He's being very frank about his political ideas and he's sticking to the text; I haven't spotted any deviations. He is trying to convince us he is a simple language teacher with radical, but harmless views. Some of his activities are out of character; in Singapore, he associated with army officers and was a member of a colonial club: a bastion of imperialism complete with colour bar. He had very odd friends for a communist."

Jack mopped his brow. "You know I get a funny feeling that I have seen a mug shot of him."

"You must have; he's been one of our clients for a long time."

"No, it's not that. Do we have a photo of him without his long hair and beard?"

"No. I believe he's had them since he was a student."

"I'd like one of him with short hair and no beard and I want to find out if he speaks Portuguese."

Maria was intrigued. "What's on your mind?"

"I've just remembered a face. Can you arrange for the photo?"

"He will have to be shorn: he won't like it."

"If he refuses to be shorn, tell him he will be shot."

Ralph added, "Prison regulations and all that."

20 The Photograph

Brian was in the VIP cell, wondering why he was there. Maria came in with Jose.

"Jose has come to give you a regulation haircut, Brian."

"No way, Jose."

"And your beard will have to go. You'll be much more comfortable in this heat."

"Get lost."

"I'm afraid you don't have a choice, Brian. I advise you to cooperate. If you don't, you will be restrained."

"And we both know what that means."

"What are you afraid of, Brian, no chin under the beard?"

"I can't remember, so one of Jose's talents is hairdressing."

"He's a very good hairdresser: he does my hair."

"In that case, go ahead, Jose; give me a style like Maria's."

"The regulation cut is short."

"I thought it might be."

"When Jose has finished, you will be taken to the photographer."

"Why, when you have got the movie?"

"What do you mean?"

"The one you are making in the interview room."

When Maria went to Jack's office, he was waiting impatiently for the photographs.

"Here they are: full face and profile."

She laid them out on the desk.

There was a hint of triumph in Jack's voice. "Look at them: is it possible?"

Ralph looked at the photos. "The likeness is frightening; what do you think, Maria?"

"If you're right, we haven't caught a big fish, we've landed a whale."

"A shark, more like; where was he last spotted?"

Ralph thought for moment. "-We aren't sure of our information. We heard he had gone to ground in Syria. Another report placed him in Baghdad, yet another, in the Yemen. The last one had him in the Sudan."

Jack went to a filing cabinet. "I should have a photo on file; here it is."

He put the photo on the desk. "There they are, side by side: see the resemblance?"

Ralph was doubtful. "It's close."

Maria was positive. "But not close enough; he'll laugh at us."

Jack spoke up. "Couldn't we confirm his identity in some other way?"

"A blood test might be the best way."

"We can get a blood sample from Brian but not from the devil in that photo. He spilt plenty of other people's blood in his time, but never his own. What are you going to do, Jack?"

"Show him the photos: we'll see how he reacts. And find out if he speaks Portuguese: if he doesn't, we are on the wrong track."

Jack went to see Brian, a pile of magazines in his hands. "I have two photos for you to look at, Brian."

"That's me, shorn like a sacrificial lamb. I recognize the other one: I've seen that photo dozens of times."

"Where have you seen him?"

"I haven't seen him; I've seen his picture in newspapers and magazines; I've even read Colin Smith's book about him."

"I've also brought some magazines for you."

"In Portuguese, I see."

"Can you read them?"

"I speak French and know some Spanish. That helps."

"But you speak Portuguese."

"Only when I'm drunk."

"What do you mean?"

"I mean I don't speak the language."

"I don't believe you; I think these photos are of the same man."

"That's wishful thinking; as usual you are inventing facts to fit your ridiculous hypothesis: that man is a homicidal maniac."

"So you don't approve of what he's done for your cause?"

"He's done nothing for our cause, but he's done a lot for yours. If you had hired him to promote your ideas, you couldn't have made a better choice. Killing innocent people never solved anything, but it gives people like you a good excuse for jumping on anyone who disagrees with you."

"An interesting theory, so you're not our man: you're as pure as the driven snow. I've never yet met a criminal who didn't plead innocence."

"I'm not a criminal. You are unbelievable; do you have to be obtuse to do your job?"

"Persistent is the word. We never give up. But I'll take a break now: you will go back to your luxury suite."

Back in his office, Jack threw the photos on his desk. "I didn't get to him, but I'm still not convinced."

Maria spoke up: "Now what do we do, Jack?"

"We carry on. Is there any news from the mountains this morning, Ralph?"

"Things have gone very quiet; perhaps it's the lull before the storm but I hope not: I want to be back in London for Wimbledon."

Jack was sarcastic. "I'm pleased to see you have got your priorities right, Ralph, but don't Wimbledon and storms go together?"

"Not every year."

The next day, Jack paid Brian a visit.

"Good morning, Brian, I trust you slept well."

"Like a baby."

"Did you enjoy your breakfast?"

"Coffee and tortillas: five-star fare."

"You see, Brian, we are humane people: you look refreshed by the good food and comfortable bed. Why did you hand the cigarettes we gave you to the guard, paranoia?"

"I don't smoke."

"But you did."

"Years ago, when I was young and didn't know any better."

"What about a cigar? These are the best: rolled on the silken thigh of a beautiful woman."

"No, thanks."

"You should support the industries of your favourite dictatorship."

Jack lit a cigar, "Smell the aroma."

"I'd prefer not to."

"You're quite right: smoking slowly kills you, but I'm not in a hurry."

"That's a very old joke."

"It still amuses me. You must relax, Brian; if you come over to us, we can make life very comfortable for you. You would stay in jail for a while, but it would be luxurious: the sort of accommodation we provide for the important drug dealers."

"You should look after your colleagues."

"Now, Brian, be sensible: most people prefer to be with us rather than against us."

"You know, Jack, for all your efforts, you have only succeeded in creating an enormous wellspring of resentment: you talk about democracy and freedom and yet you prop up totalitarian regimes."

"Get real, Brian. There's more to life than democracy; there's the little matter of the economies of the developed world. We have to secure our energy supplies: we don't want some fundamentalist megalomaniac holding us to ransom."

"That's what it's really about, isn't it: oil? The problem is if you screw down the cap on the legitimate aspirations of the mass of people, you end up with an explosion and a lot of people get hurt."

"Don't worry about that, Brian; we can always persuade rulers to do the right thing."

"By persuade, you mean bribe: come on board and we'll forgive your country's debt and open a Swiss Bank account for you."

"That's one way."

"And if you don't come on board, we'll do what we want to do anyway."

"That's right, Brian: when you are protecting the global economy, there's no room for compromise or fine feelings."

21 The Storm

Brian was surprised when Maria came to see him in the evening. "-I've brought our dinner, Brian."

"Our dinner?"

"That's right. I'm eating with you."

"Wonderful. I hate eating alone."

Maria placed a tray of food on the table.

"Jack is furious with you."

"That's his problem."

"He's furious with me too."

"Should you be talking like this? What about the cameras?"

"As usual, they're on the blink: all the surveillance cameras are out."

"And why should Jack be angry with you?"

"He has decided that my methods are useless; I'm too soft: he thinks we should have used tried and tested procedures."

"You mean torture?"

"That's right."

"Well, I'm very grateful …"

Brian was examining the laden tray of food when the cell was shaken by a huge explosion, followed by the crash of falling masonry, clattering against the cell door: the light went out.

"What the hell was that?"

"You must be used to this sort of thing, Brian. The emergency lighting operates on batteries: it will kick in at any moment. There you are: we have light."

"You're very calm."

"There's no point in panicking."

"What do you think it was?"

"I know exactly what it was: someone has blown in the perimeter wall; these cells are near it. The explosion has brought down the roof over the steps leading down here. I told you some time ago that you couldn't be sure that you would be safe down here."

"So you did: shall we leave?"

"Look through the grill in the door: what can you see?"

Brian peered through the grill. "It looks like a beam has fallen against the door: there's also a lot of rubble."

"Try opening the door."

Brian pushed against the door. "It won't budge."

"That's because it opens outwards; we'll have to wait until they dig us out."

"Shall I shout for help?"

"Don't you dare! Whoever set the bomb may not be too well disposed towards us."

"So what do we do?"

"I'll check the luxury en-suite bathroom to make sure we have water and the usual facilities."

Maria went into the bathroom and ran a tap. "We have water. What about the air? The extractor fan is dead of course."

"No problem: there's a draught through the grill in the door."

"Excellent. Now I'll check our supplies: we may be here a long time."

"You brought a lot of food."

"Yes, I did, didn't I? It's a good thing I did. I'll put some tortillas aside; they'll keep, and so will the fruit; the sweet potatoes and corn will also be for later.

The avocados are ripe: we'll eat them to start with; we can have one tortilla each."

"And to follow, Madam?"

"It's Miss. To follow, we have grilled steak."

"My favourite!"

" I'm glad you like it."

"Is that a bottle of red wine I see before me?"

"It is indeed, my lord."

"A veritable feast, my lady."

Maria set out the plates, glasses and food and Brian poured out two glasses of wine.

"Why do you use these rooms, Maria?"

"They are very secure."

"They may be secure but there's no natural light."

"That's the whole point. There's no difference between day and night down here: an inmate doesn't know how long he's been here. Do you?"

"I would say about three weeks."

"And you would be wrong. You have been here a month."

"And here I am entombed with a lovely lady."

"That's enough of that. Remember that you are the prisoner and I am the jailer."

"You're smiling. You are very relaxed, Maria: any particular reason?"

"Jack has made it quite clear that I have outstayed my welcome here: he'll ask for me to be replaced."

"Will you be sorry?"

"Yes, I will. I've been here a year and the inmates have benefited from humane treatment and good medical care. I don't want to be replaced by a sadist who thinks the Hippocratic Oath is a Greek swearword. When a prisoner is tortured he will eventually confess to anything the questioner suggests: I don't see the point of that."

"Are you sure that you are working for the right side, Maria?"

"I'm quite sure I am, Brian."

"Another glass of wine?"

"Thank you."

Brian poured the wine. "That's the last of the wine."

"It calls for a toast. Here's to freedom."

"I'll drink to that."

They clinked glasses. Brian sat back in his chair, replete with the best meal he had had in months. "The dinner was delicious. Not a bit like the usual fare."

"That's because I prepared it."

"Thank you."

"You're welcome."

Brian screwed up his courage. "Since we are alone and unobserved, would you mind if I asked you a question?"

"Go ahead."

"Forgive me for asking but how old are you?"

"Ten years younger than you, Brian."

"And you never married?"

"No. I'm married to my profession."

"Like a nun?"

"You could say that."

"How did Jack come to recruit you?"

"He didn't. I approached him."

"You wanted to work here?"

"Yes. I've already told you why."

"So you have."

"Now it's my turn. Why did you divorce, Brian?"

"Ah! I keep forgetting that you have my file. You know all about what I've done and what I haven't done."

"Answer my question."

"I really don't know. I suppose it's because Sylvie got very involved in the hotel business. I didn't like the trade and stuck to teaching. I started traveling on my own; we just drifted apart. I'm convinced that is how it usually happens."

"I think you are probably right. That's why I am still single."

"You don't like men?"

"Not very much. It is usually men who make a mess of things."

"And women don't?"

"In this part of the world they don't have the opportunity."

"Could I ask you for a big favour? Could you get a message to my parents? Just let them know I'm alive."

"I'll think about it."

"I see you have a watch, Maria. What time is it?"

"Midnight. I can't hear anybody digging: it looks as though we are going to be here for the night."

"We should get some rest. Take the bed; I can sleep on the floor."

"In the circumstances, let's not have any false modesty: it's a big bed."

"Big enough for two: I wondered about that."

"The really big fish who collaborated were allowed conjugal visits, hence the king-sized bed."

"If you really wouldn't mind."

"I'm sure you will be a perfect English gentleman."

The next morning, Brian and Maria were still trapped in the underground cell. Maria came out of the bathroom.

"Your turn, Brian. The water's cold, but then it always is. We need to be refreshed and ready to meet our rescuers. I'll get breakfast while you shower."

"Thanks. About last night, I ..."

"Don't mention it, Brian, this is a new day."

Brian went into the bathroom and sang as he showered. "Oh what a beautiful morning, La, La, La, La, La, La, La."

The shower stopped and, after a while, he emerged. "Any sign of our rescuers?"

"I heard a faint noise. I think they are starting to remove the rubble."

Maria hummed the same song as she set the table.

"What's for breakfast. Maria?"

"Tortillas, sweet potatoes and fruit. No coffee, I'm afraid: we'll have to make do with water."

"You really should have a coffee maker put in here: after all it's the VIP suite."

"I'll see to it, Sir. And while I'm doing that, would you like a mini-bar?"

"That would be nice. I would look forward to entertaining my visitors."

"Eat your breakfast."

"Yes, Mother. What do you think happened last night?"

"You mean the explosion?"

"Yes, Maria. What else could I be referring to?"

"The guerillas came to rescue their comrades: they were in the main prison."

"How many were there?"

"Only three: they were due to be executed in a couple of days."

"I see. Do you think they were successful?"

"I imagine so. The guards wouldn't put up any resistance."

There was a racket outside the cell as rubble was cleared.

"Rescue is on the way, Brian, and the electricity is back on."

"What a pity; I was beginning to feel quite at home."

They heard Jack shouting at the prison officers. "Move that beam and clear the rubble from the door."

"From the sound of his voice, Jack is in a bad mood."

"He will be when he sees me here."

The door scraped open.

"Maria! So you were here all the time. I thought you had been abducted."

"Sorry to disappoint you, Jack."

"Is the cell habitable?"

"Perfectly."

"The entrance will soon be cleared: he can stay here. Come with me."

22 The Lancandon Mountains

The mood in Jack's office was serious. Ralph looked tired and pale. "What a night!"

Maria sat in the armchair. "What happened, Ralph?

Jack filled her in. "We were here in my office when the bomb went off. I saw men in ski masks pouring through the hole in the wall. The guards couldn't get their hands in the air quickly enough and Ralph couldn't hide in that cupboard quickly enough."

"So there was no resistance? What did they want?"

"The three men we caught a year ago; the guards simply opened their cell and let them go."

"And the other prisoners?"

"Still here; the guerillas weren't interested in common criminals. The whole show only lasted half an hour: it was perfectly planned. I'll leave you two for a moment: I want to talk to our guest."

Jack went down to Brian's cell. "I've decided to give you to the specialists in the capital. Perhaps you will be happier talking to them. I can see that I am wasting my time with you. We have a flood of defectors coming to us from the Eastern Bloc: so many that we can choose only those from the highest echelons. I'm going to debrief them."

"The rats are leaving the sinking ship."

"That's about the size of it, Brian. But they can be talkative rats and very useful to us."

"You know you have no right to hold me."

"Might is right in this day and age. Your new inquisitors are going to find out what you know about the guerillas. I'm confident they will have much more success than me: they don't have my humanity. Pack your bag: we move tomorrow morning."

Jack stomped out and a few minutes later, Maria arrived.

"Maria! What a nice surprise. Have you come to bid me farewell?"

"So Jack has told you."

"Yes. I'm moving to a new hotel in the capital."

"You're going by road to the airport. The route goes through the mountains. Whatever happens, don't move a muscle: Jack would love to put a bullet in your back and say that you tried to escape. There could be armed elements on the road so be careful and don't take any risks."

"You're being very mysterious, Maria."

"Let's say I wouldn't like to see you killed."

"So you care what happens to me?"

"You know I do. Let's leave it at that for the moment."

Early next morning, Brian was taken from his cell into the yard. The bright sunlight hit his eyes. Jack and Ralph were waiting near a camper.

"Here's your transportation,"

"A camper truck: a bit battered, isn't it, Jack?"

"You don't judge a sword by the scabbard, Brian; it's armour plated and the windows are bullet proof. The engine is special: it can outrun anything on these roads. Put your bag in the back."

Brian was pushed into the front.

"Where do I sit?"

"Between Ralph and me."

Ralph closed the door and Jack clipped a handcuff on Brian and fastened it to a seatbelt anchor.

"Now I'm tethered. What happens if we crash and the truck catches fire?"

"You burn. Let's go."

The engine roared into life as Ralph drove off. "There's Maria, waving us off."

Jack was grumpy. "I should never have taken on a woman; she's been completely useless: turned the prison into a summer camp for juvenile delinquents."

Brian smiled. "What would you have preferred, Jack: a concentration camp for minorities?"

"That's about it: I'm tired of bleeding heart do-gooders."

"You're tired of a lot of things, Jack."

"I'm certainly tired of you and you can stop calling me Jack: in fact you can stop talking to me at all."

Ralph tried to calm Jack down. "Take it easy, Jack, we have two hours of road in front of us."

"Why they never built an airport nearer to the town beats me."

"Money, Jack. Very little of it trickles down here from the capital. Why didn't you request a chopper?"

"Because I would have been given one of the local army death traps; I prefer to take my chances on the road."

"We should be safe; we have a police escort up ahead."

Brian looked back. "And one is following us."

Jack was apoplectic.

"What? I didn't request a police escort."

"Well we've got one and the car in front is slowing."

Brian looked back. "And the one behind is closing."

Jack was furious. "Slow down; I know what's going on: they see a camper truck and they think: tourists. They intend to stop us, accuse us of some infraction of their non-existent highway code, and take a bribe to forget about it. What a country!

The camper slowed to stop behind the leading police car. Jack got out and marched to it. "I'll sort them out. Do you know who you are dealing with?"

The Mexican pointed his revolver at Jack's head.

"Yes, Jack. I know who you are. I'll take your pistol."

Jack's jaw dropped. He tamely handed over his pistol.

"Thank you; now get in the police car."

Ralph was aghast. "The policeman is pointing his revolver at Jack's head. What the Dickens is going on?"

Brian nudged Ralph. "There's also a policeman on your side. He's pointing a gun at your head."

Ralph was indignant. "Now look here! You'll be sorry for this."

Ralph got out and Brian rattled his handcuffs. "Could you get the key for these? The man over there has it."

The Mexican walked across to the camper. "Hello, Brian. Here's the key."

"Thanks. How are you, Marco?"

"Never better. Is this Jack's briefcase?"

Marco opened the briefcase and rifled through the contents. "Here's your passport and your wallet." He checked the contents of the wallet. "You have money and this is your air ticket to the capital. When you get there, don't leave the airport. Go straight to the Mexicana desk.

There's an air ticket waiting for you. Take the next available flight."

"Yes. Thanks, Marco."

"That's all. You can drive that camper, can't you?"

"Yes. What's going to happen to Jack and Ralph?"

"Nothing bad. We'll hold them for a few months and then release them in exchange for talks with the government."

The police cars climbed into the mountains. Jack was as white as a sheet.

"Where are you taking us?"

"You'll see, Jack."

Ralph was calm. "You're not the police, are you?"

"Just for the day, Ralph."

"How is it you know our names?"

"You're famous. Or at least you will be."

The cars slowed down and turned down a narrow track. Jack was worried. "Why are we turning off the main road?"

"We live up there."

"In the mountains?"

"We're climbing. Haven't you noticed?"

The cars came to a stop. Marco ordered them out of the car. "This is as far as the cars can go: our escort is waiting here." He beckoned to a young man. "Watch them, Jose."

Ralph was appalled. "Is that who I think it is, Jack?"

"Yes, that's Jose; the ungrateful pup!"

"Your HQ had a mole, Jack! No wonder the guerillas knew their way about. Who can you trust these days?"

The guerillas busied themselves with the cars.

"What are they doing now, Jack?"

"You will have noticed that we are near a cliff. There is a volcanic lake below. They're getting rid of the cars."

There were shouts, followed by two splashes as the cars were pushed off the cliff into the lake.

Marco came to them. "Now we walk."

23 The Rainforest

Marco and his men set off in Indian file along the narrow forest track, with Jack and Ralph in the middle. The forest was alive with the sounds of birds and, occasionally, an unidentified animal. Jack, carrying his extra weight, was very distressed and panting as he struggled to keep up. "How much further? We've been walking for hours. I've been stung by every insect known to science and I'm exhausted."

Ralph was unfazed. "Cheer up, old chap. They are probably going to kill us, so it doesn't matter if you get malaria or some other nasty disease."

It was late afternoon when they arrived at a village nestling under huge trees.

Marco announced the good news. "We're home."

Ralph and Jack sank to the ground; Ralph heaved a sigh. "Thank goodness; is that collection of miserable huts your HQ?"

"It is. Come into the conference room. Jose, bring water for our guests."

Jack addressed Marco. "So you're the chief honcho."

"I have that privilege. Come in and sit down. Here's Jose with the water."

Jose grinned at Jack and Ralph as he poured water.

"I apologize for the tin cups but we have few luxuries."

Jack gulped water down and held his cup out for more.

"You haven't been trained very well, Jack. Don't guzzle water when you are dehydrated."

"Thanks for reminding me. What do you intend to do with us?"

"You will stay with us while I am negotiating with the government. You will not be harmed. As you can see, your accommodation will be basic, but these huts are built from local materials and are quite comfortable. The hammocks are first class. The open sides of the huts allow the cooling mountain breeze to enter: we particularly enjoy the evenings. Do you guys play chess?"

Ralph spoke up. "I do."

"Then you won't be bored. Chess is our main recreation up here: it sharpens the intellect and helps with tactical planning. If you try to escape, you will be shot. The government won't know whether my two pawns are alive or dead: you will still be bargaining counters."

Ralph smiled. "That's good to know."

Jack spoke up. "What about poker?"

"A game can be arranged but you won't win, Jack, we have all the aces."

"Why did you let the third member of our party go?"

"He was no use to us."

"He was one of your people."

"No. He was an innocent, but rather rash tourist."

"How do you know that if you have never seen the man before? You're just trying to cover for him."

Marco did not respond.

"So he's still active. I was right all the time. I should have eliminated him when I had the opportunity."

"In your situation, that's a foolish thing to say, Jack. "

Ralph intervened. "Do you have television up here?"

"Yes."

"Satellite channels?"

"Of course. We have to keep up to date with world events."

"You wouldn't be interested in tennis?"

"I love tennis. Am I right in thinking you want to watch Wimbledon?"

"You are indeed."

"No problem. We have a good chance in the ladies' singles this year: you won't miss a match."

"That's very generous of you."

Jack was furious. "Stop kissing the man's feet and remember who you are."

"At this time of year, Jack, I'm a tennis fanatic."

A month later, Ralph and Jack were washing their clothes in the stream which ran through the village. Marco emerged from his hut. "You guys enjoying the tennis?"

"First class. It's rare that I get to see every match: too busy, usually."

"What about you, Jack? Are you still sore because I beat you at poker?"

"Sure I am: I always was a bad looser."

"How do you guys stand in the chess league, Ralph?"

"If the table I see posted is correct, I'm tenth and Jack is twentieth and last."

"You know your problem, Jack? You're too impatient: you move too quickly and make mistakes."

"Is that so?"

"It must be a national flaw. I see you jumping into action all over the world: you don't study the board and history is a dead letter for you."

"How did you reach that conclusion?"

"I'll give you an example: Vietnam. If you had studied the board, you would have seen that the French lost too many pawns. In the end they had to resign. Your country jumped in and made exactly the same mistakes. Checkmate. The list of countries you have messed up is endless: Cambodia, Indonesia, Guatemala, Cuba, Chile, Nicaragua, Panama, Grenada, Libya, Lebanon, Angola, Mozambique, Somalia ... "

"You're overstating your case."

"Perhaps I am. But you have stirred the pot in most parts of the world. All you have succeeded in doing is antagonizing their populations. In the end, you will reap the whirlwind."

"If you think you are going to prevail, have another think, Buddy. Is your puny band of terrorists capable of achieving anything?"

"We are not terrorists. We have never killed anyone: our aims are political and, in the end, the government will have to listen to us."

"How do we figure in your grand plan?"

"We have used you to get the attention of three governments and we have only just started."

"What exactly are your political aims?"

"They are very simple: land reform and social justice for the indigenous population. Gentlemen, I must leave you; I have a campaign to plan. Have a nice day."

As he was walking away, Ralph said, "Have a nice day."

Jack was annoyed. "Are you crazy? Have a nice day! Where do you think we are? Taking an ecological vacation? Studying the flora and fauna of this verdant land?"

"As a matter of fact I am. I always loved camping with the Scouts."

"Are you out of your mind? We should be planning our escape."

"You can plan your escape, but I'm staying. I'm fed up with my old life: poking into people's private lives. It disgusts me. I'm going to make television documentaries: the private lives of wild animals. I intend to be like David Attenborough; he must be about ready to retire. I can imitate his breathy tones as I creep up on mountain gorillas."

"You should be thinking about getting away from these mountain guerillas."

"That was a pun, Jack."

"Was it? I'll try not to pun again."

"It's the men's semi-finals tonight. Shall I wake you?"

"Wake me and I shall add you to the list of extinct species."

Jack and Ralph were sitting at a rustic table in front of their hut, taking breakfast.

"More coffee, Jack?"

"Thanks. And I'll have another tortilla. Don't take all the guacamole."

"Sorry. I am a greedy-guts, aren't I?"

"Yes, you are."

Ralph poured more coffee. Jack sipped.

"How long have we been here, Ralph?"

""Exactly ten weeks.

"That long? This idea of yours, Ralph: making documentaries. Do you reckon it would work?"

"Of course it would work. What have we been doing these last years?"

"Observing and interviewing people; keeping notes; making video and sound recordings."

"Exactly."

"What do you know about animals and things?"

"I have a degree in zoology."

"You do? I didn't know that. So you are an expert."

"I wouldn't say that. But I know enough to do the popular stuff."

"And you have that Limey accent: just right for voiceovers."

Ralph was surprised. "Don't tell me you are interested."

"Maybe. What about the economics of a business like that?"

"No problem. My old man has pots of money. He would take a share. "I'm not short of a bob or two in my own right. You must have put away quite a bit."

"You've no idea how much I've fiddled in expenses."

"I can guess."

"What's the market like for documentaries?"

Ralph leaned forward. "Work it out. How many channels do we get here?"

"I've never counted."

"All those channels need programmes: thousands of hours of programmes. If we get any more channels, they'll be showing paint drying."

"What about staff and equipment?"

"We'd need a cameraman and a sound engineer and a pickup truck. We can rent the lot as and when we need them. Are you coming in?"

Jack took the last tortilla. "I'll think about it."

Ralph and Jack had constructed a leafy roof to shade their table. Jack had managed to get a sketchpad and pencils from Marco and Ralph was reading a book he borrowed from the camp library.

"It's been very quiet the last few days, Jack."

"That's because Marco and half his merry men have left the compound."

"What do you think they are up to?"

"No good as usual."

"You're very preoccupied. What are you writing?"

"It's a storyboard, like they do for the movies."

"Can I see?"

"Go ahead."

Ralph flicked through the pages of the sketchbook. "These drawings are brilliant. I didn't know you could draw so well."

"My violin de whatsisname."

"Ingres."

"Whatever."

"But art was his profession. Playing the violin was his hobby. Your hobby is art."

"Stop nitpicking: you know what I mean."

"Does this signify that you're interested in my documentary project?"

"I could be. It just gave me an idea for cartoons."

"Cartoon production is too labour intensive: rows and rows of illustrators drawing and colouring: the investment is enormous."

"I saw a computer programme on my last visit to the big house. Some of the nerds were playing with it: they were creating figures that moved, they called it computer animation."

-How interesting. I've heard of that. I've even seen an example, but the figures are very wooden."

"Look at my storyboard. It's about a kid's toys that come to life. Wooden toys would look wooden, wouldn't they?"

"I suppose they would."

"Your problem, Ralph, is that you don't see the wood for the trees."

"Jack! You made a joke!"

"So what! Look what's coming."

Marco and his men trooped into the village.

"A bunch of our friends. They look happy."

"Hello, Jack. Hello, Ralph."

"Have you been up to some kind of mischief, Marco?"

"And what mischief, Jack! We occupied the town for a whole week: it was like a fiesta, a carnival."

"And nobody objected?"

"Objected? They loved it. They were too busy getting their faces onto the television networks to notice that we were emptying the armoury."

"So you got some exposure."

"Our masked faces and our demands will be seen and heard by half the world and it didn't cost us a peso. What are you doing?"

"I'm about to call a board meeting. Jack and I are going to start a business."

"Fine. I'm dying for some breakfast. See you after your board meeting."

Marco went over to the canteen.

"As I was saying, Ralph, the rate at which software is developing, we'll see full-length computer-animated features within the next five years. I want to get in on the ground floor."

"What about my ideas for documentaries?"

"We can do that too. What subjects did you have in mind?"

"See the butterfly on that bush? It's a Monarch. It would make a fascinating programme."

"It would be a short programme. Butterflies are ephemeral. That means they only live for a day."

"A common misapprehension, Jack. That butterfly has travelled thousands of miles to get here."

"That so? I thought we could do something more interesting, like the Commode dragons in Indonesia."

"Komodo, Jack. They've been done to death."

"What about mountain gorillas?"

"Likewise."

-Dinosaurs?

"Extinct."

"With computer animation we could resuscitate them."

"That's a brilliant idea."

24 Plans

Jack and Ralph were reclining in their hammocks enjoying the sunset and listening to the rainforest fauna.

"Do you know how long we have been here, Jack?"

"No. You're the one who keeps the diary."

"It'll be a three months next Tuesday."

"Time flies when you're having a good time."

"It does indeed, and you've stopped talking about escaping. Have we been brainwashed?"

"You mean like Patty Hearst?"

"She's a good example."

"No, we haven't been brainwashed. We haven't picked up AK47s and joined the ranks of the rebels. We've discovered that we're basically lazy. We like lolling in our hammocks listening to the forest and watching the sun set. People pay good money for a vacation like this. They call it eco-tourism."

Ralph sat up. "Eco-tourism. That would make a good subject."

"Put it on the list."

Marco came out of the headquarters hut.

"I've just come off the satellite phone. Good news, you're going home."

Ralph rolled out of his hammock. "What's happened?"

"The government people are going to talk to us. I leave for the capital next week."

Jack was doubtful. "Do you trust them?"

"No. But all the media will have the news and I will have a laissez-passer signed by the president."

"In that case, we can explore the forest."

Marco was surprised. "Aren't you going to rush back to your offices?"

"No. We're both resigning."

"To do what?"

Ralph pointed to the forest. "We'd like to make a documentary about this place. Judging by the noises we hear, there is abundant wild life."

"Feel free. Personally, I'm ready for a few creature comforts in the big, bad city.

We're closing down the camp. If you're going to make a movie, you will need some equipment."

"We'll do the research first."

Jack added, "Then we'll hire the technical guys to shoot the movie."

"I wish you luck. Tonight we celebrate. As our honoured guests, you are invited to a party: lots to eat and drink, thanks to the generosity of the Las Casas shopkeepers. We've even kidnapped a Mariachi band for the evening."

Ralph and Jack were shooting material for a documentary. During their captivity, Jack had shed many kilos. Ralph had added a few to his spare frame. They were back at the village taking tea.

"The shoot isn't going very well, is it Jack?"

"This is the movie business, Ralph. You can't expect it to be plain sailing."

"I suppose not. But the cameraman keeps complaining that his lens is fogging up with the humidity and the soundman is useless."

"I got rid of him. I'm doing the sound from now on."

"You're supposed to be the director, shouting 'cut' and so on."

"No problem. I'm recording everything on my Nagra. That's just for local colour. We'll do your voiceover after we've done the cutting."

"More tea?"

"Thank you."

Ralph poured. "Did you listen to the World Service news?"

"No. Anything new?"

"Apparently Marco has done a deal with the government, which is going to pump billions of pesos into land reform and so on."

"I'll believe it when I see it. What about that place we looked at in the town?"

"The old Spanish house? I love it, Jack."

"Do you think we should buy it? It's very cheap."

"Jolly good idea. I'd like a *pied a terre* to call my own."

"So would I. We should buy it before we throw away our savings on the movie business. We could restore it to its pristine state and take guests."

"A hotel?"

"An eco-lodge, something like the Na-Bolom in Las Casas."

"You mean the tree-huggers' guesthouse."

"Yeah. In another age I would be very suspicious of that lot."

"We've changed, Jack. Any day now, we are going to start hugging trees and campaigning for indigenous rights."

"We should take only the well-heeled who are bored with the usual vacation spots. You can run eco-tours and show them the wild life."

"Brilliant idea."

"But we are going to finish this movie if it's the last thing we do."

25 Reunion

Brian is sitting on the terrace of a hotel in a Caribbean island. He was thinking about going back to his apartment when he got a shock: Marco and Maria, who was carrying a baby in her arms, came onto the terrace.

"Maria!"

"Hello, Brian. You know Marco."

"Of course. Hello, Marco. And a baby, Maria. How old is he? She?"

"He's three months old."

Brian mastered his emotion. "What are you doing here?"

"I came to see you. Marco very kindly escorted me. He's on an official visit to his old friends on the island."

Marco smiled. "How did you get on after you left us?"

"It went a smooth as silk. I drove the camper to the airport and parked it. I took the plane to the capital and transferred to a flight, which brought me here."

"I'm sorry that we had to keep you in the dark for so long, but the negotiations with the government were delicate and protracted. You can correspond with your parents now."

"I'm glad about that. The old folks must be sick with worry."

Maria spoke up. "No. I wrote and told them a long time ago that you were safe and well."

"Thank you, Maria. Do you think I'll be able to visit them?"

"Eventually. You can't get direct flights from here, but there are plenty of indirect routes."

Marco got up to leave. "Well, I'll leave you two. Good to see you again, Brian."

"Good to see you, Marco."

When Marco had left, Brian and Maria looked at each. Finally Maria spoke. "-It's been a long time, Brian."

"It's been an age. Have you known Marco long?"

"I've known him since I was a child."

"I met him on my first visit to the mountains, quite by accident."

"I know. You stumbled on his base."

-"t took me a while to convince him that I was just a tourist."

"The problem was you saw the location of his base and how few men he had. He was trying to give the government the impression that he had an army."

"I gave my word that I would keep quiet. To show my good faith, I delivered a consignment of medical supplies on a second visit."

"And after your second visit, Ralph had you picked up."

"I'm glad he did. It meant I met you. I thought I heard Ralph's voice the other day. I was in the bar and the TV in the lounge was on. I could swear it was Ralph going on about butterflies."

"It would be Ralph. He and Jack have resigned: they're making documentaries."

"Well I'm ..."

"Their employers are convinced they have been turned. They wrote a final report clearing you of any suspicion of being a spy."

"Which happens to be the truth."

"I visited them at their hotel; they call it an eco-lodge. Ralph conducts eco-tours in the mountains. Jack has mellowed; he's lost all his flab and he leads an ascetic life. He's become a thoroughly nice man. They have restored a vast, old Spanish house. It even has a chapel, which they've decorated with religious pictures and statues looted from churches during the various revolutions. Jack has become an autocephalous bishop, complete with purple robes and mitre."

"Is that legal?"

"Yes. Anyone can declare himself autocephalous. It simply means independent. I attended a service. Jack was magnificent in his robes. The congregation, mainly matrons from Texas, adored his sermon on brotherly love."

"What about you? Are you still intent on protecting your borders?"

"I had you fooled, didn't I? I had everybody fooled. I was the inside contact for Marco and his merry men. Jose was the other mole."

"So you knew I wasn't a spy. In the circumstances, you were quite hard on me."

"I had to play the game; otherwise Jack would have been suspicious. And you did know Marco's location and how small and ill equipped his group was. I had instructions to slip you a lethal potion if you started to crack."

"Would you have done it?"

"No. I took the Hippocratic Oath. I persuaded Marco to arrange for you to leave the country; if you had stayed your life would have been in danger."

"All I have ever done is flit from country to country."

"Like a butterfly."

"And as a result I have been hounded by the security services of several countries."

"Once they get an idea in their heads, they don't give up."

"I've noticed."

"Well you're safe now. How do you find the island?"

"I love it. I'm doing some teaching."

"You're not living in the hotel?"

"No. I have a nice apartment on the seafront. I come here most evenings for a sundowner."

"You know that Hemmingway often stayed here?"

"It's the hotel's proudest boast: hardly an evening goes by without someone reminding me."

They were silent for a while. Brian looked at the baby. "Baby is very good. Can I hold him?"

"Sure."

She passed the baby to Brian who smiled.

"Are you and Marco a couple?"

"No. And we never have been."

"Do you know what? Baby reminds me of my father. What's his name?"

"Brian. And he reminds you of his grandfather."

Brian's eyes popped.

"Don't drop him!"

"You mean to say…"

"Yes, Brian. It happens. It has happened to some of the best people."

"Anthony Burgess for one. This is wonderful. I must tell my parents."

"I've already told them."

Brian and Maria left the hotel and went to his apartment on the sea front.

There was hardly any traffic in the city. Only the sound of the surf and a few voices in the street broke the silence.

"Your apartment is lovely, Brian. And the view from your balcony is superb."

"I'm glad you like it. I have a question for you. Would you ..."

"No, Brian. We talked about this. Do you remember?"

"I do. You were unsure about marriage."

"Not any more: ours will be in two weeks' time. Agreed?"

"Agreed."

"You do realize that you will have a wife and child to support?"

"There goes my easy life. I'll have to settle down and work full time."

"Even a butterfly stops flitting from flower to flower at some stage in its life, Brian."

www.ingramcontent.com/pod-product-compliance
Lightning Source LLC
Chambersburg PA
CBHW070851290526
45795CB00001B/77